Mosdos Press
Literature

OPAL

SUNFLOWER I

Mosdos Press
CLEVELAND, OHIO

Mosdos Press

Educators transmitting appropriate values and academic excellence

Copyright © 2013 by Mosdos Press.

All rights reserved. Printed in Israel. Second Printing.

No part of this publication may be reproduced or distributed in any form or by any means, or stored in a database or retrieval system, without prior permission in writing from Mosdos Press, 1508 Warrensville Center Road, Cleveland Heights, Ohio 44121.

Part One
ISBN-10: 0-9858078-6-5
ISBN-13: 978-0-985-80786-3

Set
ISBN-10: 0-9858078-3-0
ISBN-13: 978-0-985-80783-2

Mosdos Press Literature

Editor-in-Chief
Judith Factor

Creative/Art Director
Carla Martin

Senior Curriculum Writer
Abigail Rozen

Copy Editor
Laya Dewick

Writers
Lessons in Literature / Jill's Journals:
Jill Brotman

Author Biographies:
Aliza B. Ganchrow

Text and Curriculum Advisor
Rabbi Ahron Dovid Goldberg

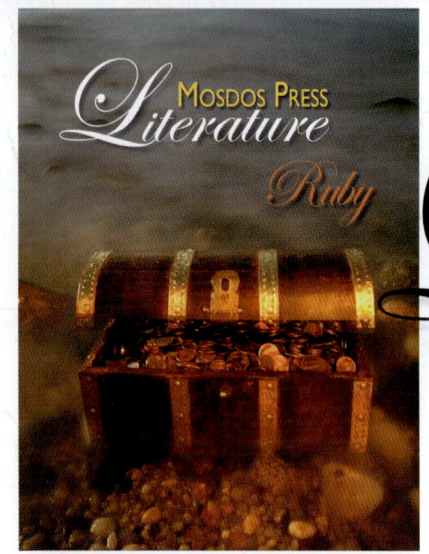

Mosdos Press Literature

Anthology Series

- Opal
- Ruby
- Coral
- Pearl
- Jade
- Gold

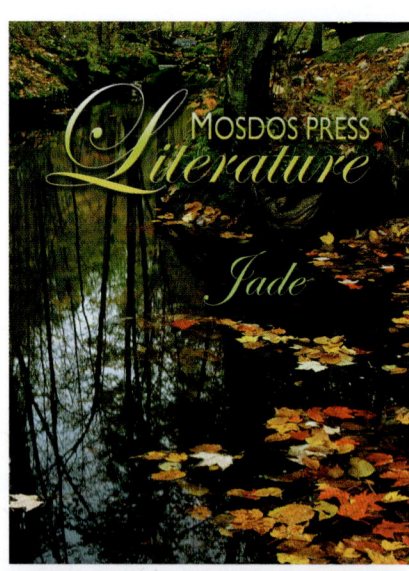

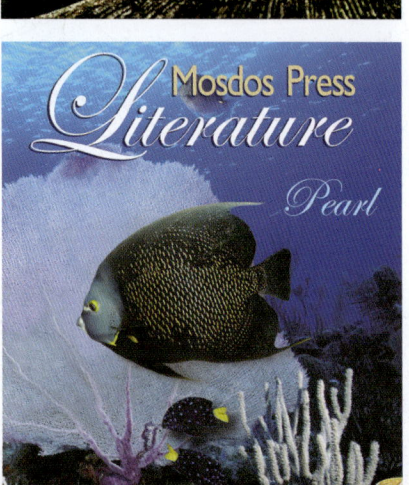

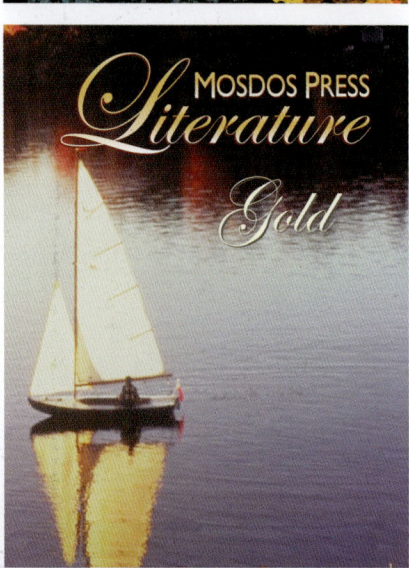

unit 1

all about the story!

Lesson in Literature	What Is a Story?	2
The Jar of Tassai	Grace Moon	4
The Secret	Emily Dickinson	16
Lesson in Literature	What Is Plot?	18
The Story of the White Sombrero	A Mexican Legend Retold by Mariana Prieto	20
Lesson in Literature	What Are Characters?	36
A Cane in Her Hand	Ada B. Litchfield	38
I Go Forth to Move About the Earth	Alonzo Lopez	48
Lesson in Literature	What Is Setting?	50
Boom Town	Sonia Levitin	52
General Store	Rachel Field	66
Jill's Journal	On Assignment in Rhyolite, Nevada	68
Lesson in Literature	What Is Theme?	72
Taro and the Tofu	Masako Matsuno	74
Unit 1 Wrap-Up		90

unit 2

all about the plot!

Lesson in Literature	What Is Internal Conflict?	96
Good-Bye, 382 Shin Dang Dong	Frances Park and Ginger Park	98
New Kid at School	Betsy Franco	116 —5
Lesson in Literature	What Is External Conflict?	118
Sybil Rides By Night	Drollene P. Brown	120
Lesson in Literature	What Is Sequence?	132
Nothing Much Happened Today	Mary Blount Christian	134
I Am Running in a Circle	Jack Prelutsky	144 — 6
Lesson in Literature	How Is Setting for a Drama Different?	146
Food's on the Table	Adapted From a Story by Sydney Taylor	148
Breakfast	Jeff Moss	158
Lesson in Literature	What Is the Main Idea?	160
Across the Wide Dark Sea	Jean Van Leeuwen	162 —7
The World with its Countries	John Cotton	178
Jill's Journal	On Assignment on the Mayflower	180
Unit 2 Wrap-Up		184 —8

unit 3

all about characters!

Lesson in Literature	What Are Character Traits?	190
The Printer	Myron Uhlberg	192
The Other Way to Listen	Byrd Baylor	202
Jill's Journal	On Assignment Visiting the Wheelers in New Jersey	206
Lesson in Literature	What Is Point of View?	210
Lorenzo & Angelina	Eugene Fern	212
Lesson in Literature	Relationships in a Story	232
A Day When Frogs Wear Shoes	Ann Cameron	234
Weather	Anonymous	246
Lesson in Literature	Cause and Effect	248
The Burning of the Rice Fields	Lafcadio Hearn	250
Until I Saw the Sea	Lilian Moore	260
Lesson in Literature	What Is Biography?	262
Mother to Tigers	George Ella Lyon	264
Dreamer	Langston Hughes	276
Unit 3 Wrap-Up		278
Glossary		283
Acknowledgments		286
Index of Authors and Titles		287

Table of Contents vii

unit 1

PEOPLE

PLACES

BRIGHT IDEAS

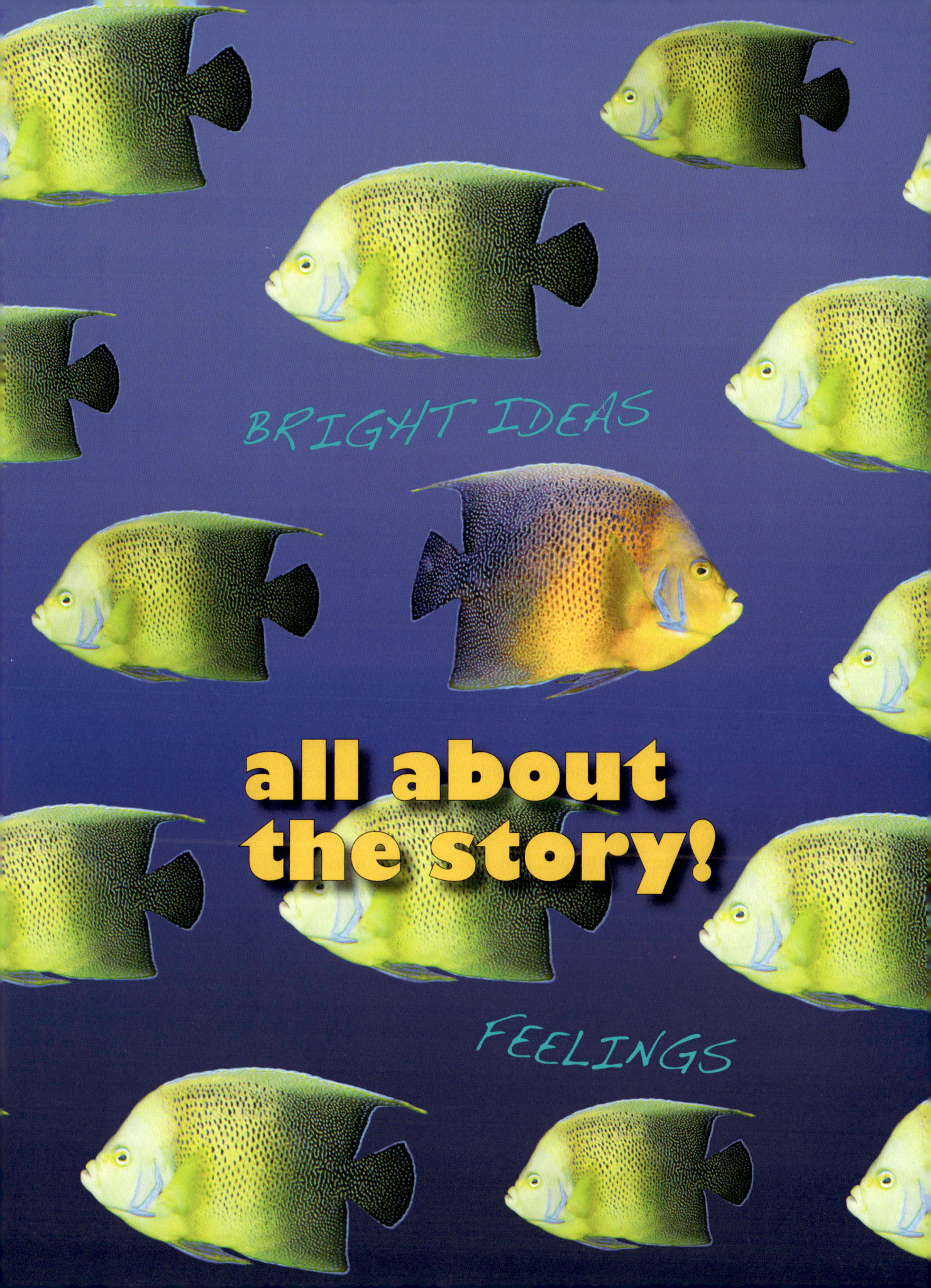

all about the story!

FEELINGS

Lesson in Literature...
TREASURE OF THE ANDES

WHAT IS A STORY?
- A **story** is about something that *happens* at a certain *time* in a certain *place*.
- What *happens* in the story is called the **plot**.
- The *people* or *animals* in the story are called the **characters**.
- The *time* and *place* in which the events happen are called the **setting**.

THINK ABOUT IT!
1. How do the boys discover the silver urn?
2. Who are the five characters in the story?
3. Where does the story take place? Name the country the boys live in, and the mountains and the lake that are near their farm.

Carlos sat on the wooden box that his father had placed near the vegetable garden. "Carlos," his papa had said, "you are such a good boy. You work so hard. Sit down sometimes!"

Carlos was nine. He smiled, remembering his father's words. He liked taking care of the potatoes, corn, and barley. He would grow up to be a farmer or fisherman just like his mama and papa.

Carlos lived in the Andes Mountains near Lake Titicaca in Bolivia. Bolivia is in South America.

Carlos knew his parents were different from other farmers. They read many books. They knew many things about the world. In fact, they had named him after a famous Bolivian artist.

Oh, to be a painter of pictures! Oh, to be a weaver of brightly colored cloth! Mama made beautiful cloth. But she didn't have much time to weave. She had to take care of the farm and his brothers and baby sister.

"Carlos! How are you?" It was his friend, Tomie, calling. "Want to search for buried treasure?"

"Sure," Carlos shouted back. Their favorite game was hunting for treasure. They had always heard stories that something valuable was buried in the Andes. They imagined finding treasure and being heroes. Then they could both go to art school. They would be famous artists! They had talked about this many times.

"You know, Tomie, I've been thinking. The legend says the treasure is where the earth is like a mirror or a sheet of glass. Well, Lake Titicaca is so calm. It really looks like a sheet of glass!"

They headed for the lake with their llama, Isabella. She wore her bright pink collar and ear tassels. Their spades were set in the pack that she wore.

Carlos and Tomie were near the edge of the lake. Suddenly, Carlos tripped on a rock and fell. "Are you all right?" cried Tomie.

"My hands are scraped, but I'm okay. It was just a big rock!"

"Hey, wait," Tomie exclaimed, as he helped his friend to his feet. "Look at that!" he said. "That's no rock. See, it's shiny—just the way the lake is shiny." They set to digging with their spades, excited. But Carlos worried. What if it were nothing special? Then there would be no art school.

Little by little they uncovered an old and heavy silver urn. "It's just like what we saw at the museum in the city," Tomie said. They attached the urn to Isabella's pack with rope. They wanted to get home quickly, but Isabella had a heavy load.

Soon they saw their mamas working in the field. The boys untied the urn. Together, they held it up for their mamas to see. "Look!" the boys exclaimed. "We found the treasure of the Andes!"

At first their mothers laughed. "Are you certain it belongs to no one else?"

"Mama," Carlos cried. "How could something so old belong to someone else?"

The two women looked at each other. "Do you know what this means for our families?" Tomie's mama said to the boys.

Carlos' mama nodded. "We have not told either of you how Tomie's little sister needs medicine, or how little food we have had to get by on. We save the food for the children."

"Thank you so much," Tomie's mama said quietly. "You are both heroes."

The Jar of Tassai

Blueprint for Reading

INTO . . . *The Jar of Tassai*

Tassai was a Pueblo Indian girl whose family lived and farmed near the desert. Like many children, Tassai had a secret. Slowly and carefully, in a secret place, Tassai was making a jar from clay. She had discovered the clay near the desert. Tassai dreamed of the day when she would surprise everyone with the beauty of the jar. Just as that day arrived, something happened! Her precious jar was endangered, but so was something even more precious. Tassai had to choose between the two in a split second. As you read *The Jar of Tassai*, ask yourself what choice *you* would have made.

EYES ON *Story Elements*

What makes a story? You would probably agree that, in a story, something has to *happen*. What happens is called the **plot**. You might add that a story must have *people*, or animals, or maybe even robots! These are the **characters**. The characters live at a certain *time* in a certain *place*, which are the story's **setting**. Finally, if the story is a good one, it will have an *idea*, or **theme**. As you read *The Jar of Tassai*, see if you can identify the plot, characters, setting, and theme.

The Jar of Tassai

Grace Moon

Tassai[1] lived on the top of a mesa[2] that looked far out over the Painted Desert.[3] The air was as clear as thin ice. It even made the faraway mountains and blue hills look nearer than they really were. Tassai was a Pueblo Indian[4] girl. She was as brown as a nut that has dried in the sun. She liked to lie on the edge of the mesa. She would look over the desert and dream long dreams.

But Tassai did not often have time for dreams. There was too much work for her to do. Tassai worked with her mother in the little fields at the foot of the mesa. It was not hard work, and it had magic in it. It had the magic of watching green things spring up out of the ground where only brown earth had been before.

---

1. *Tassai* (TASS EYE)
2. A *mesa* (MAY suh) is a flat area at the top of steep mountainsides.
3. The *Painted Desert* is a desert in Arizona, east of the Colorado River.
4. The *Pueblo* (PWEB lo) *Indians* are Native Americans who live in the American Southwest. The stone or adobe houses they live in are also called *pueblos*.

Tassai brought water, too, from the spring at the foot of the mesa. She carried it up the steep trail in jars. For hours each day she ground the red and blue and yellow grains of corn. She cooked when her mother needed her help. She also knew where to find the grass that her mother wove into baskets.

There was one thing Tassai did that no one knew about. This was because she did it only at times when no eyes were watching. She was making a jar from clay that she had found in a secret place. There the earth was smooth as honey to the touch and dark in color. Not even her mother knew that Tassai was working at this jar. It was Tassai's secret.

She shaped it and smoothed it. She knew how to do this from watching her mother. The most beautiful jar of all started to form itself in her hands. She painted fine black lines on it and baked it a golden brown. Tassai thought that there had never been a jar as lovely as this one. She carefully wrapped it in a blanket and put it away in a safe place.

All through the hours while she worked in the fields, Tassai thought of her jar. In her thoughts a little song sang itself over and over again until her feet danced to the music of it:

It is so beautiful,
My big, round jar!
So round and beautiful!
Only the Moon,
When it walks on the edge of the world
Is like my jar.
Round and smooth it is,
And has a shine that sings!
Maybe the Moon has come to me
To be my jar!

Not long before Tassai made her jar, the Governor of the Pueblo called the people of the town together. They gathered in the little open place where meetings were held. He told them that the people of three towns were going to meet for a time of dancing and feasting. He asked that each man, woman, and child bring to the feast something he or she had made. Prizes would be given for the very best things brought to the feast.

Everyone was very excited about the Governor's news. There was much talking and planning of what should be done. Tassai was excited from the first. She could hardly wait for the time to come.

The day itself was wonderful. There was a feel in the air that was different. Tassai felt that she could not walk or talk or even breathe as she did on other days. The open place in the town was bright with color. It was like a fair.

There were good smells and different sounds everywhere. There were baskets and pottery and woven things all spread out for everyone to see.

There were silver bracelets and rings and belts. There were bright blankets and things of leather and wood. There were ears of corn that were bigger than any Tassai had ever seen before. There were beaded shoes and nets for carrying things. There were little cakes made of pine nuts and seeds. There was good food cooking in pots.

Tassai was one of the very last to come into the open place on that big day. She had been busy since sunup, helping her mother. At last she was free. She picked up the blanket in which her jar was wrapped and ran to the open place. There she stood, holding the blanket close to her side.

The Governor of the Pueblo moved from place to place with some elderly people. They looked long and closely at each of the many things that had been brought. With them was a visitor from a nearby town. He had come with his little daughter to see the dancing and feasting.

The little girl danced ahead of them as they walked. She looked at everything with bright eyes.

When the people had seen everything else, they started walking up to Tassai. She was nervous now. Maybe they would not think her jar was beautiful. Others began to gather around. They had not known that Tassai would have anything to show.

"Maybe it is not very good," she said in a voice that was so low no one heard her. "Maybe it—" Then her words would not come at all.

When she opened the blanket, the beautiful jar was not there. She had not noticed that there were two piles of blankets in the room of her home. The one she had picked up in her hurry held only an old corncob doll.

There was a big laugh from those who stood near. The words of Tassai, explaining what she had done, were lost. Quickly she pushed her way through the laughing people and ran home. She did not know that the little girl had wanted to see that doll again and was following her.

The house of Tassai was the last one in the little town. It was on the very edge of the mesa top. She ran into the door. She did not notice that the little girl who had followed her had stopped suddenly just outside the doorway. The child was watching, with wide eyes full of fear, a snake that picked up its head from behind a big stone. It was a rattlesnake. It moved its flat head closer and closer to the little girl. She gave one loud cry as Tassai came out of the door with the jar in her arms. Tassai had thrown off the blanket and held just the jar in her arms.

There was no time to think. There was no time to call for help. Tassai did the only thing she could do. With all her might she threw the jar at the rattlesnake. It broke into many pieces on the rock, and the snake lay flat and still.

The little girl did not make another sound. Her father, who had heard her first cry, came running. He held her in his arms.

For the first second, Tassai thought only that the rattlesnake was dead. Then she thought of her jar. No one would call it beautiful now. She picked up a little broken piece. As she was looking at it, the father of the little girl took it from her hand.

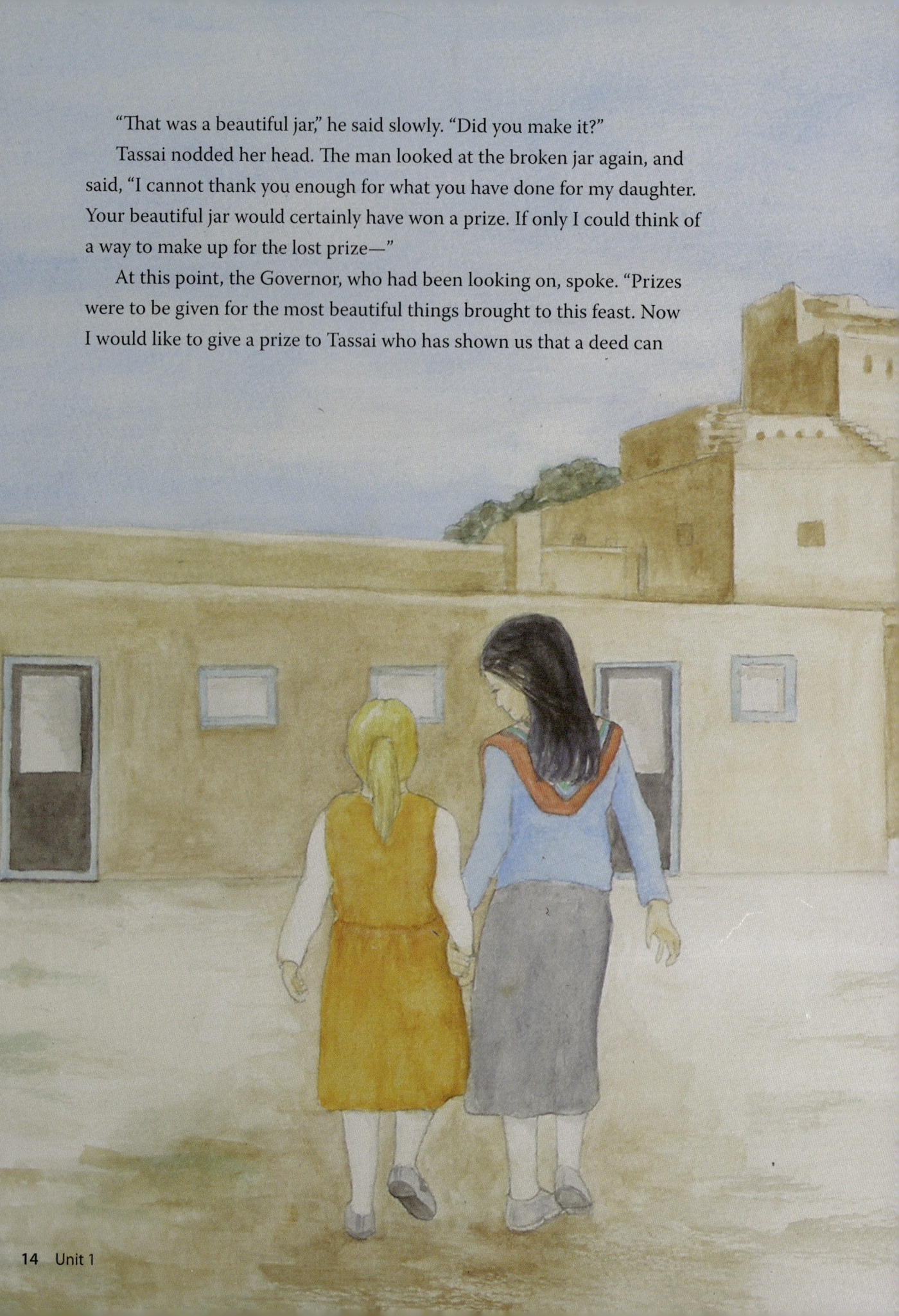

"That was a beautiful jar," he said slowly. "Did you make it?"

Tassai nodded her head. The man looked at the broken jar again, and said, "I cannot thank you enough for what you have done for my daughter. Your beautiful jar would certainly have won a prize. If only I could think of a way to make up for the lost prize—"

At this point, the Governor, who had been looking on, spoke. "Prizes were to be given for the most beautiful things brought to this feast. Now I would like to give a prize to Tassai who has shown us that a deed can be very beautiful, too." With this he handed her a prize. The elderly people nodded their heads with pride. The children who were gathered around clapped and cheered.

The little girl whom Tassai saved came up and smiled at Tassai. She asked, "Can I see your pretty corncob doll again?" Tassai held out her hand to the little girl and soon they were walking together toward Tassai's house. Now Tassai felt very happy. It did not matter that her jar was broken. She could make another, even more beautiful.

About the Author

Grace Purdie Moon always loved Indians. When she was a little girl, she thought she actually was an Indian since she was born in Indianapolis, Indiana! She and her husband, Carl Moon, who was an artist, spent years traveling in Indian Country, living with different tribes and gathering material for their work. Grace Moon is famous for her paintings of Indian children. She wrote 19 books, and her husband illustrated all of them. They even authored some of these books together.

The Secret

Emily Dickinson

We have a secret, just we three,
The robin, and I, and the sweet cherry-tree;
The bird told the tree, and the tree told me,
And nobody knows it but just us three.

But of course the robin knows it best,
Because he built the — I shan't tell the rest;
And laid the four little — something in it —
I'm afraid I shall tell it every minute.

But if the tree and the robin don't peep,
I'll try my best the secret to keep;
Though I know when the little birds fly about
Then the whole secret will be out.

Studying the Selection

FIRST IMPRESSIONS
Would you have been able to think as quickly as Tassai did?

QUICK REVIEW

1. What work did Tassai do secretly?
2. What did Tassai hope to do with her jar?
3. Why did Tassai leave the feast and run home?
4. How did Tassai's jar get broken?

FOCUS

5. At the end of the story, Tassai felt very happy, even though her jar was broken. Why did she feel this way?
6. Every story has a plot, characters, a setting, and a theme, or main idea. Copy the chart below onto a piece of paper and fill in the empty boxes.

List three characters	1. 2. 3.
List two settings	1. 2.
List two important things that happen in the story	1. 2.

CREATING AND WRITING

7. In the story, the Governor gave Tassai a prize for doing a good deed. What do you think it was? Imagine that you are the Governor, and write a letter to Tassai that describes the prize and thanks her for her brave deed.
8. Tassai loved making her jar. At home, find an empty jar. Clean it well and decorate it. Fill it with something you like, such as candy or small pieces of a game.

The Jar of Tassai 17

Lesson in Literature...
THE THREE SISTERS

WHAT IS PLOT?
- What happens in a story is called a **plot**. A plot has a beginning, a middle, and an end.
- At the *beginning* of the story, a problem is presented.
- In the *middle* of the story, things happen and changes occur that may solve the problem.
- At the *end* of the story, the problem is solved.

THINK ABOUT IT!
1. What problem does Mom have?
2. What does Mom do that may solve the problem?
3. Why do the girls stop bickering at the end of the story?

The three sisters were triplets. Their names were Annie, Sara, and Dina Smith. They lived with their mom and dad and two younger brothers, Jake and Sam. Their house was on a pretty street with lots of trees.

Not all triplets look alike, but these three girls looked just like each other. And, of course, they were the same age—eight years and four months, to be exact.

It seemed they didn't think the same way about anything. They spent a lot of time bickering. Even when they agreed with each other, they argued about things like who agreed first. Or who looked more like the other. Or who was born a minute or two earlier.

Then their mother would say, "Girls girls girls!"

Once they had a disagreement about who had fallen asleep first the night before. Even Dad said irritably, "How do they know if they were asleep?"

Mom looked for activities that they would like to do *together*. One Sunday afternoon Mom said, "Here's an idea that is just right for you: a vegetable garden called the Three Sisters!"

"Was it named after us?" asked Annie.

"You? Who would name a garden after you?" answered Sara.

Mom said, "This is what the Iroquois Indians did. It is the perfect garden. The three vegetables go together and help each other, just the way you three do."

"Huh?" said the triplets.

18 Unit 1

"Well, sometimes," sighed Mom.

"So what are these sisters?" asked Dina.

"The Three Sisters," said Mom, "are corn, beans, and squash."

"But we don't like beans or squash," protested Annie.

"I like beans!" exclaimed Sara.

"And I like squash. At least I think I do. Well …" Dina said, "Mom, what's squash?"

"But why these vegetables?" interrupted Annie.

"The Three Sisters go together because corn is a grain. It's also a carbohydrate. Beans are protein. And squash gives you vitamin A."

"What does that mean?" asked Dina.

"It means you get all the food groups you need. But also the Three Sisters go together because the colors are pretty, and the vines of the beans can grow up the corn stalks. The squash shades the soil. The beans provide nitrogen, which the corn needs. So the Three Sisters take care of each other." Mom sounded like a teacher.

They all went out back to pick a place for the garden. Of course, Sara, Annie, and Dina each pointed in a different direction and shouted, "Here!" "No, there!" "You're both wrong. Right here!" But Mom picked the site. The plants needed sunlight six to eight hours a day.

The next Sunday they dug up the soil. They put something in the earth to help plants grow better. They planted their seeds. They felt so good after working in the sun. Mom had gotten a tiny picket fence to put around the plot. It looked just right!

Each day after school, the girls went out to look at their garden. They were very excited when little green sprouts began to stick up from the ground.

Two months after the planting, Sara became sick with the flu. Annie and Dina were upset. How would Sara do her share of the gardening?

"Mom," cried Annie and Dina. "What are we going to do? Sara's too sick to do her share! It's not fair."

Mom said, "What is not fair is that Sara feels so sick, and she is worried about her plants. What do you think we should do?"

Annie and Dina looked puzzled. Suddenly Annie said, "Hey Dina. I have an idea." She took Dina's hand. They headed for the back door.

An hour later, Mom looked outside. Annie and Dina were checking the plants and weeding in Sara's part of the garden.

When they came back into the house, they brought some of the flowers from Mom's garden. "Is this all right, Mom?" asked Annie.

"We probably should have asked first," said Dina, "but these are for Sara."

Mom almost cried. "You girls are just like your plants. You are the three sisters who can count on each other."

Blueprint for Reading

INTO . . . *The Story of the White Sombrero*

Sombreros, tortillas, ponchos—Mexico! You can almost feel the hot sun as you read this story. Andres and Francisco are two brothers who live in the Mexican hills. One day their mother asks them to go to the marketplace and sell some sombreros she has woven. The brothers agree, but along the way, so many funny things happen that you might wonder if they will ever reach the marketplace. After you have read some of the story, you will see that each brother has his own way of solving a problem. See if you can predict what each brother will say as new problems come up. Were you right?

EYES ON *Plot*

A **plot** is what happens in a story. A good plot has a *beginning*, a *middle*, and an *end*. The beginning introduces the story and makes you want to keep reading. The middle is where exciting or interesting things happen. The end completes the story. Between the beginning and the end, something must change. The change may be that a problem is solved or that a character learns to act differently. As you read *The Story of the White Sombrero*, see if you can spot the place where one of the characters has changed.

THE STORY of the WHITE SOMBRERO

A Mexican Legend
Retold by Mariana Prieto

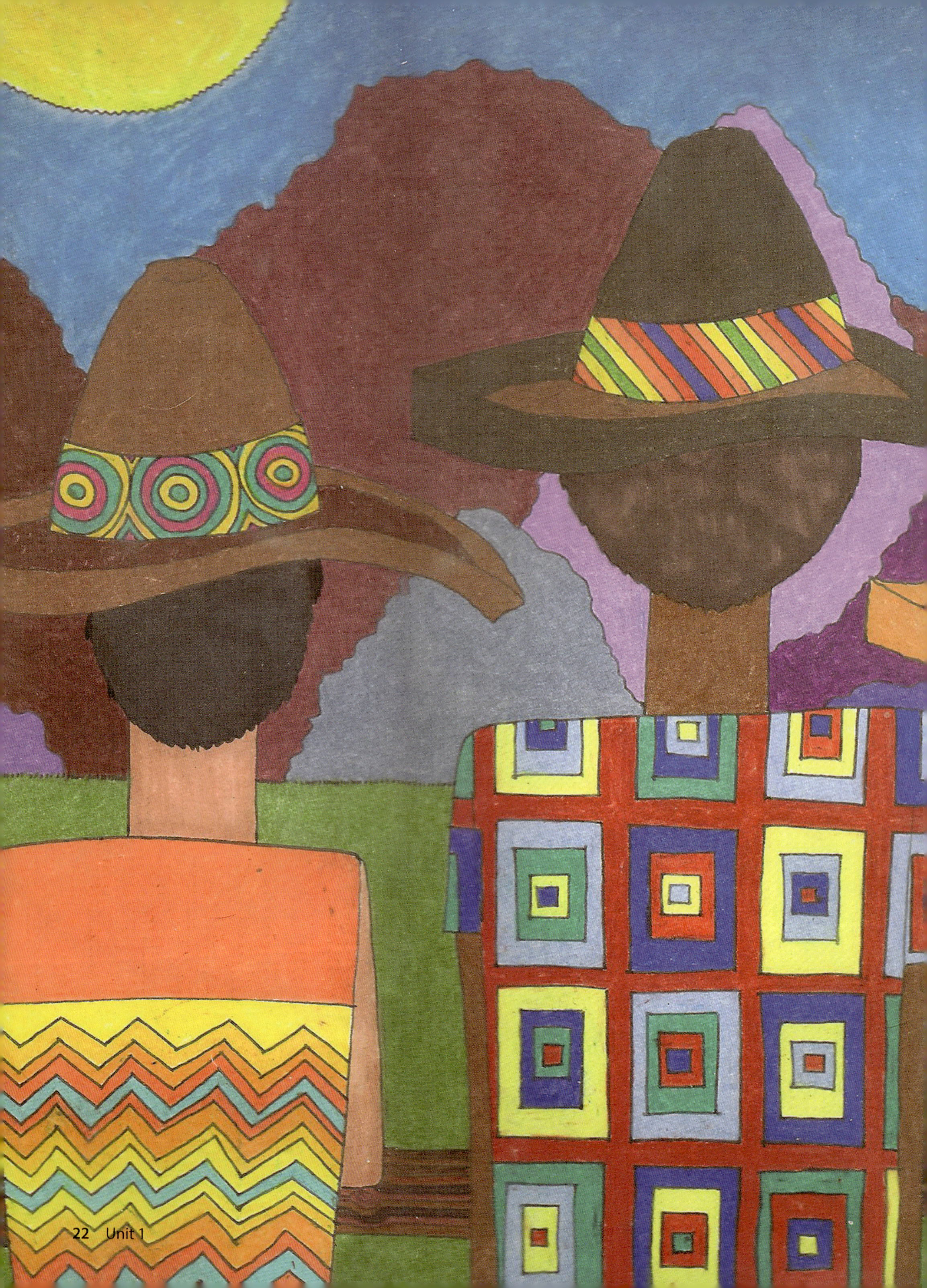

Once long ago, in the hills of Mexico, lived two brothers. One brother was named Andres.[1] He was short and round like a lima bean. The other brother was named Francisco. He was long and thin like a string bean. They lived in the country where wheat is grown.

Their mother, like all the other women, wove broad-brimmed hats, called *sombreros*.[2] She wove them from *paja trigazo*,[3] or wheat straw. She and their father always took the sombreros to the market to sell. But one day she decided the boys should make the journey.

"You are old enough to take the sombreros to market," she told them. "Your father and I have work to do here."

"*Bueno!*"[4] Andres said. "I am brave. I know we can make it all right." His big black eyes were bright and sure.

"I do not know, Mama," Francisco said anxiously. "The way is long and many things can happen." He waved his long, thin arms hopelessly.

"Don't be silly," Andres said. "We can get there all right. If we have trouble, I am sure we will find someone to help us."

So they went and got their little burros and piled the sombreros high on the backs of the animals. When they had tied the sombreros in place, they climbed on their burros and started off for the market.

It was a long, hot ride, but Andres sang as he rode. He might not have, had he known what lay ahead for them.

---

1. *Andres* (ON dray)
2. *Sombrero* (sahm BRAIR oh)
3. *Paja trigazo* (pah SHAH TRIH GAH SO)
4. *Bueno* (BWAY noh) is Spanish for "good."

> **WORD BANK**
>
> **burro** (BURR oh) *n.*: a small donkey used to carry loads

The Story of the White Sombrero

When night came, the boys made camp. They tied the burros to nearby orange trees.

"I saw a wasp fly by," Francisco said. "There must be nests in those trees. Surely the wasps will sting our burros and something terrible will happen."

"Nonsense," said Andres. "If there are wasps flying around, they will keep thieves from stealing our sombreros."

The boys untied the mountains of sombreros from the burros and placed them nearby. Then, after feeding their animals, they ate some cold *tortillas*. Finally, they rolled themselves in their ponchos and went to rest on the ground. Soon they were fast asleep.

Word Bank

poncho (PAHN cho) *n.*: a cloak that has an opening in the middle so that it can be pulled over the head and worn around the body

They slept until daybreak. The birds calling and singing woke them.

"We must get an early start," Andres said.

So they got up and placed the sombreros on the backs of the little burros.

They had just tied the piles of sombreros and returned to roll up their ponchos, when the wasps came.

The wasps attacked the burros. The burros brayed in fury and dashed about. The boys wanted to help, but they were afraid of getting stung, so they stayed at a safe distance.

In their panic, the little burros broke the ropes that tied them to the trees. As the wasps stung them, they were like wild bucking horses, not mild little burros. The cords that held the sombreros in place broke, and the sombreros spilled all over the ground, while the boys rushed about picking them up.

Suddenly overhead in the orange trees, a terrible chattering began. The trees were filled with monkeys.

Word Bank
brayed *v.*: sounded the harsh cry of the donkey

The Story of the White Sombrero   27

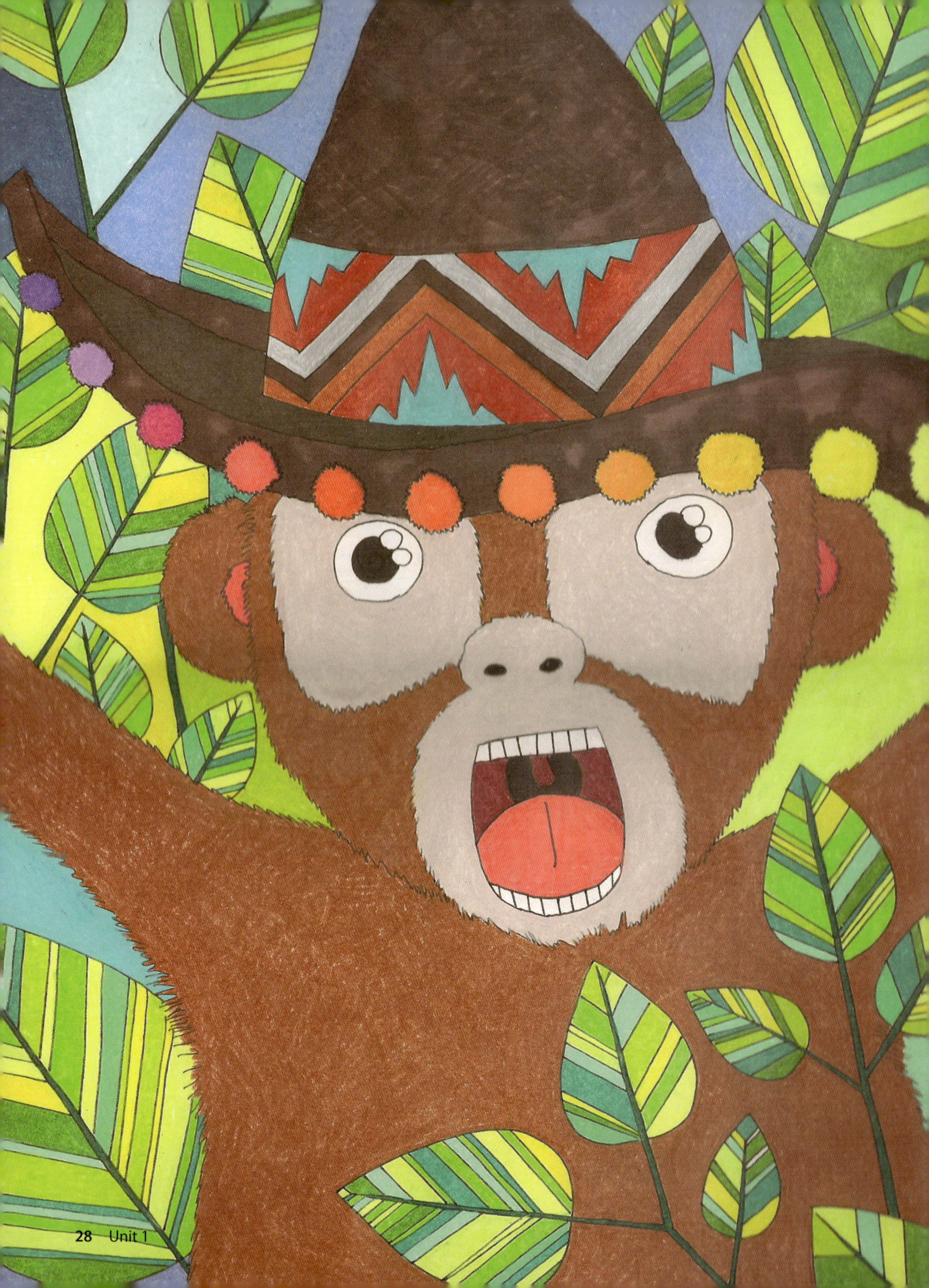

The monkeys, seeing the sombreros on the ground, scurried down the trees and began gathering them up. They put the sombreros on their heads, laughing and chattering to one another.

"Now we're in real trouble," Francisco said. "What are we to do?"

The little burros, in the meantime, had galloped down to a nearby stream. They rolled in the water and drowned the wasps. But Andres and Francisco did not solve their problems so easily.

The boys picked up some pebbles and threw them at the monkeys. The monkeys in turn picked oranges from the trees and threw them at the boys. But they went on grabbing sombreros.

The oranges plopped to the ground. They broke open and splattered the sombreros that lay there. The boys, too, were splattered with juice from the same oranges.

"We are in a hopeless state," Francisco said. "Let's go home."

"No, no," said Andres, as he kept on throwing pebbles.

At that moment, an old man came along. He stared in surprise at the strange scene.

The monkeys swung from tree to tree, wearing the sombreros and tossing them back and forth to each other.

"Chee, chee," Andres screamed at the monkeys. "*Vaya*, go."

"Keep on throwing pebbles," he ordered Francisco.

The Story of the White Sombrero   29

At last the monkeys seemed to tire of their game. Some of them took off the sombreros and tossed them to the ground. But others went leaping away into the dense, green thicket, still wearing the hats. When they were gone, the boys began picking up the sombreros, which were all spotted and sticky with orange juice.

"I told you it was hopeless," Francisco said.

"You give up too easily," said Andres. "Let's take these sombreros down to the stream and wash them."

The old man watched as the boys gathered up the sombreros, and shook his head. He followed the boys to the stream.

The boys found their burros by the stream. When they saw that the burros were all right, they tied them to trees and gave them some sugar. Then they began to wash the soiled sombreros. They washed and washed, but they could not get the sombreros clean.

> **WORD BANK**
>
> **thicket** (THIK it) *n.*: a group of bushes or small trees growing closely together

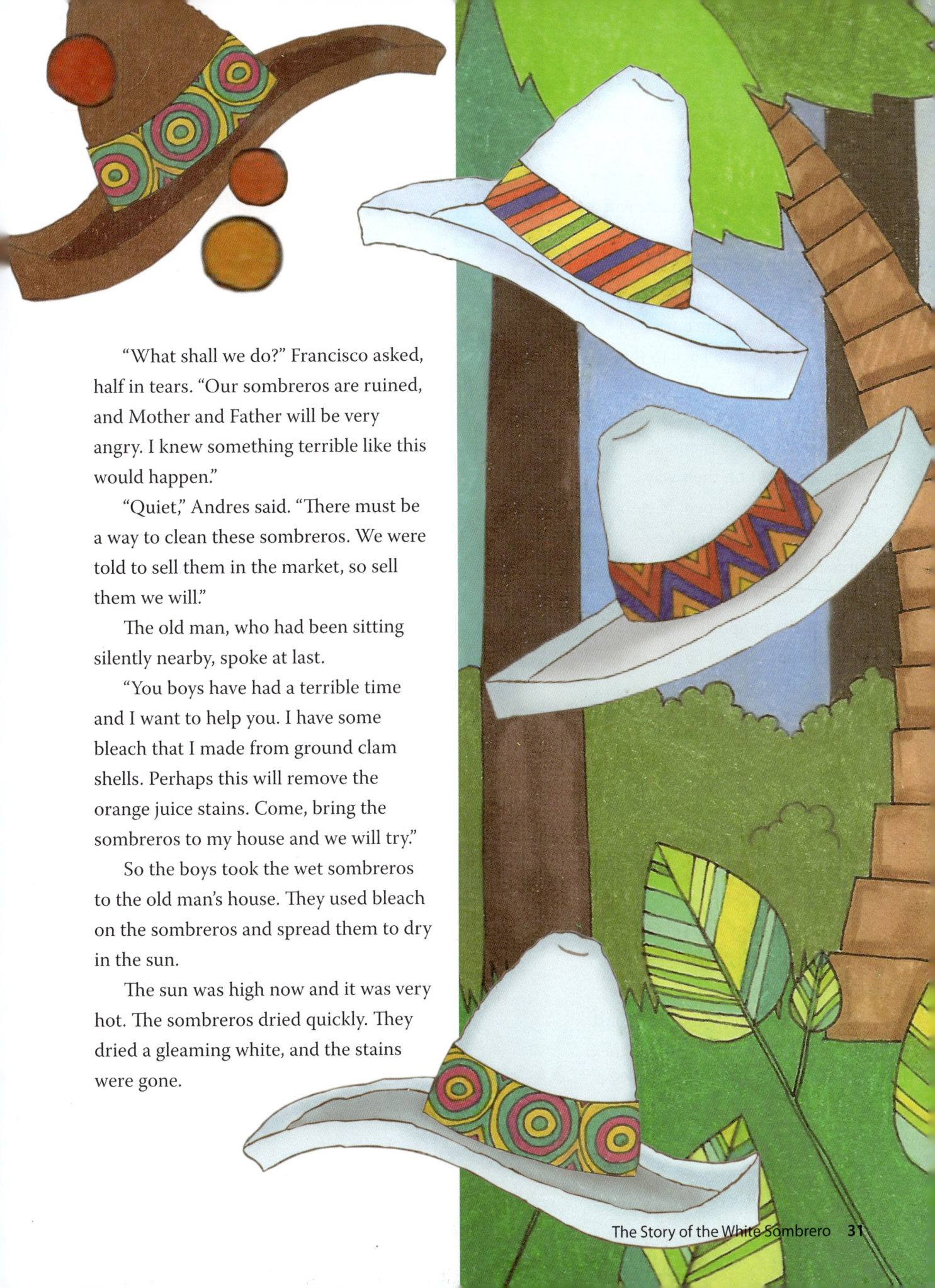

"What shall we do?" Francisco asked, half in tears. "Our sombreros are ruined, and Mother and Father will be very angry. I knew something terrible like this would happen."

"Quiet," Andres said. "There must be a way to clean these sombreros. We were told to sell them in the market, so sell them we will."

The old man, who had been sitting silently nearby, spoke at last.

"You boys have had a terrible time and I want to help you. I have some bleach that I made from ground clam shells. Perhaps this will remove the orange juice stains. Come, bring the sombreros to my house and we will try."

So the boys took the wet sombreros to the old man's house. They used bleach on the sombreros and spread them to dry in the sun.

The sun was high now and it was very hot. The sombreros dried quickly. They dried a gleaming white, and the stains were gone.

The Story of the White Sombrero

"Oh, no," said Francisco. "Look at our sombreros now! They don't look like the sombreros that other people make. Surely, no one will want them."

"We will try to sell them anyway," said Andres. "Come, help me load them on the burros."

So they walked back to the stream with the sombreros and fastened them to the backs of their burros. Then they thanked the old man and went on their way.

At the market, people gathered around the boys when they unloaded their sombreros. No one had seen such white sombreros before. The people liked them and they all wanted to buy them. Almost at once, the boys had sold all of their sombreros.

When the boys were home again, they told their mother and father what had happened to them. Andres told the secret of how they had bleached the sombreros. And Francisco told how quickly they had sold them.

Their parents decided from that day on to bleach all of their sombreros. They sold them as fast as they could make them and they all became very rich.

The Story of the White Sombrero

One afternoon, while they were working, Francisco said to Andres, "You had the courage to keep on trying. That is why our trip was a success. In spite of all that happened, we came out well in the end because of your bravery. I should have been the brave one, because I am older. But from now on, little brother, I am going to be as brave as you are."

He smiled and picked up one of the sombreros and put it jauntily on his head.

And they both laughed.

And so ends the legend that is told by the people in Mexico who make sombreros.

Word Bank

jauntily (JAWN tih lee) *adv.*: worn easily, happily, and a tiny bit proudly

ABOUT THE AUTHOR

Mariana Prieto was born in Cincinnati, Ohio in 1912. She lived and studied in many Spanish-speaking countries and these experiences inspired the settings of many of her books. Mrs. Prieto contributed over 600 articles and short stories to newspapers and magazines. Besides for writing, she worked as a radio broadcaster, librarian, and creative writing teacher. She also taught Spanish to Air Force officers. Mrs. Prieto liked painting, people, cooking, history, and animals.

Studying the Selection

FIRST IMPRESSIONS
Have you ever heard the expression "monkey see, monkey do"?

QUICK REVIEW
1. Why were the brothers going to the market?
2. What happened when the wasps stung the burros?
3. What did the monkeys do to the sombreros?
4. How did the old man help the brothers?

FOCUS
5. How was Andres' personality different from Francisco's?
6. What happens in the story is called the plot. A plot can usually be summed up, or *summarized*, in a few sentences. Copy the following chart onto a piece of paper, and, using the helping words, write one sentence next to each word. When you have done so, you will have a summary of the story's plot.

Market	*Example:* Two brothers were sent to the market to sell the sombreros their mother had made.
Wasps, burrows	
Monkeys, oranges	
Old man, bleach	
Sell, money	

CREATING AND WRITING
7. In the story, wasps sting the burros, the burros run away, monkeys grab the sombreros, monkeys throw oranges, and more. Do you think you could write one more episode for this story? It should fit into the story right after the part where the two brothers put the bleached sombreros out to dry. Write about some funny thing that happens to the brothers, the burros, or the sombreros before they reach the marketplace. Ask your teacher if some of the students can read what they have written aloud.

8. Sombreros are big Mexican hats. If you own one, bring one to school for 'Hat Day.' If you don't have a sombrero, bring a hat that is unusual in some way and tell the class why it is special.

The Story of the White Sombrero

Lesson in Literature...
THE SPANISH SHIPS

WHAT ARE CHARACTERS?

- The **characters** are all the people in the story. Some stories have animal characters, or even robot characters.
- The most important characters in the story are called the **main** characters.
- The main characters may change because of what happens in the story.
- An unimportant, or **minor**, character usually remains unchanged throughout the story.

THINK ABOUT IT!

1. What quality does Jerry have that most people notice first?
2. What does Uncle Jack say that makes Jerry feel differently about himself?
3. Jerry has lots of qualities other than stuttering. What do you think some of his other qualities are?

I'm Jerry Gooding. I guess the most important thing about me is that I stutter. I have other qualities, too. But stuttering is the first thing that people learn about me, as soon as I open my mouth.

What does stuttering mean? Well, my dad says there are three types of stuttering. Sometimes I repeat part of a word, like when I asked my brother yesterday, "W– W– W– Where are you going?" I had trouble getting from the *w* to the rest of the word. My brother hates it when I stutter.

The second type of stuttering is sort of like the first but it's more of a hiss. It happened last night. I had to get to basketball practice. "Mom," I said, "*SSSS*ave me *sss*some dessert, please." My oldest sister says I sound like a snake when I do that. Of course she never heard a snake speak.

Mom asked when I would be home. This leads me to the third kind of stuttering. It comes in the middle of a sentence. I said, "I'll be back about— *uh hum, uh like*—seven o'clock." I don't know why I said it that way.

My doctor says that stuttering runs in families. My father's father—my grandpa—stuttered when he was a kid. He still stutters a little. Nobody can get mad at him for stuttering, because he's Grandpa! What could be more special?

Why do I stutter? I know what I want to say, but I have trouble saying it. People think I'm stupid because I stutter. Tommy at school makes fun of me. That just makes me stutter more. I also stutter when I'm excited or tired.

Mom and Dad say that most kids who stutter get over it. They *outgrow* it. My Uncle Jack says that lots of famous writers stutter. "So what if they stutter?" he declares. "They're geniuses! What about the presidents who stuttered? George Washington! Thomas Jefferson! Theodore Roosevelt!"

Uncle Jack is shouting at this point. "And Thomas Jefferson wrote the Declaration of Independence, practically by himself! And what about Winston Churchill? None of these guys gave up because of a little stuttering!"

When Uncle Jack talks this way, of course it makes me feel good. He is funny, too. He tells me, "Practice saying this. This is what Winston Churchill said over and over to get rid of his stutter. *The Spanish ships I cannot see since they are not in sight. The Spanish ships I cannot see since they are not in sight.*"

I tell Uncle Jack, "None of the kids I know ever heard of Winston Churchill. Who else stuttered?"

"The president of Pepsi Cola. Some famous basketball players."

That sounds pretty weak to me.

Uncle Jack gets serious. "This is not such a bad problem. And, it makes kids tougher. You need to work hard on this. That means ignoring the people who hurt your feelings. You also have to relax and take your time when you speak."

I think about Uncle Jack's words that night. I decide I have to feel good about me. I need to slow down and be more patient with myself. I am going to start practicing with the Spanish ships. I get so much support from Mom, Dad, Uncle Jack, and Grandpa. I am even going to ask my brother and sister to help me help myself.

> The Spanish ships I cannot see since they are not in sight.

Blueprint for Reading

INTO . . . *A Cane in Her Hand*

What is the difference between a problem and a challenge? A *problem* is a difficulty that a person has. It could be a health problem, a learning problem, or any one of hundreds of other problems. A *challenge* is a difficulty too, but it is a difficulty that is more like a test, or even a dare. In sports, one group will challenge another to a game of soccer. It is as though the first group is saying, "We are hard to beat! Let's see how good you are at this game!"

When people have difficulties in real life, some people call them "problems" and feel very unhappy. They do not feel they can overcome their difficulties. Other people say, "These are not problems, they are challenges!" When you begin to read *A Cane in Her Hand*, you will meet a girl named Valerie Sindoni who has a problem. As you continue reading, you will see her change her problem into a challenge. Ask yourself, "How does she do that?" The answer will be valuable to anyone who has a problem.

EYES ON *Character*

Characters are the people in a story. Sometimes the author tells us what the characters are thinking; other times we have to figure that out ourselves. There are as many types of characters as there are real people. As you read *A Cane in Her Hand*, try to imagine how Valerie feels at different points in the story. Do you know someone who has a challenge like hers? When you think about that person, it will help you understand Valerie. When you read about Valerie, it may help you understand the person you know just a little bit better.

My name is Valerie Sindoni, and I don't use my long cane all the time.

Sometimes I don't need it. I don't need it when I go to Roger's house. He's my cousin and lives next door. I've been there so many times, I know every step of the way.

Why do I have a long cane? Because I can't see very well—that's why. But I haven't always had a cane.

I *have* always worn thick glasses to help me see. But one day I found that, even with my glasses, I wasn't seeing well.

I couldn't find my new clothes when I got up. I banged into the door and hurt my knee.

After breakfast, I went outside. I saw something moving in Roger's yard. It was Roger with his little sister Ruthie behind him. They were coming out of a gray fog. "That's strange," I thought. I knew it wasn't a foggy day.

I ran toward them. But I stubbed my toe and fell.

"Hey," Roger yelled. "Look where you're going. You blind or something?"

Ada B. Litchfield

A Cane in Her Hand

"I guess so," I said, pushing myself up and feeling around for my glasses.

To tell the truth, I *was* having trouble seeing. Everything kept disappearing in a fog.

Ruthie said, "Don't worry, Val. Let's play."

But I was worried. I had a sharp pain in my left eye.

Like the fog, the pain came and went.

"I'm going home," I yelled at Roger.

"Hey, Val!" Roger bellowed, chasing after me. "Come back and play! I didn't mean that about being blind."

"Forget it," I told him and ran into my house and slammed the door.

My mother was worried when I told her about the pain. She made me go to my room and lie down. "Rest your eyes," she said. "I think the pain will stop."

After she helped me to bed, I heard her go downstairs and call my father and the doctor.

I didn't go to school on Monday. Instead, I went with Mom and Dad to see Dr. King. He was glad to see me, and that made me feel better. He took me into a room where he'd tested my eyes before.

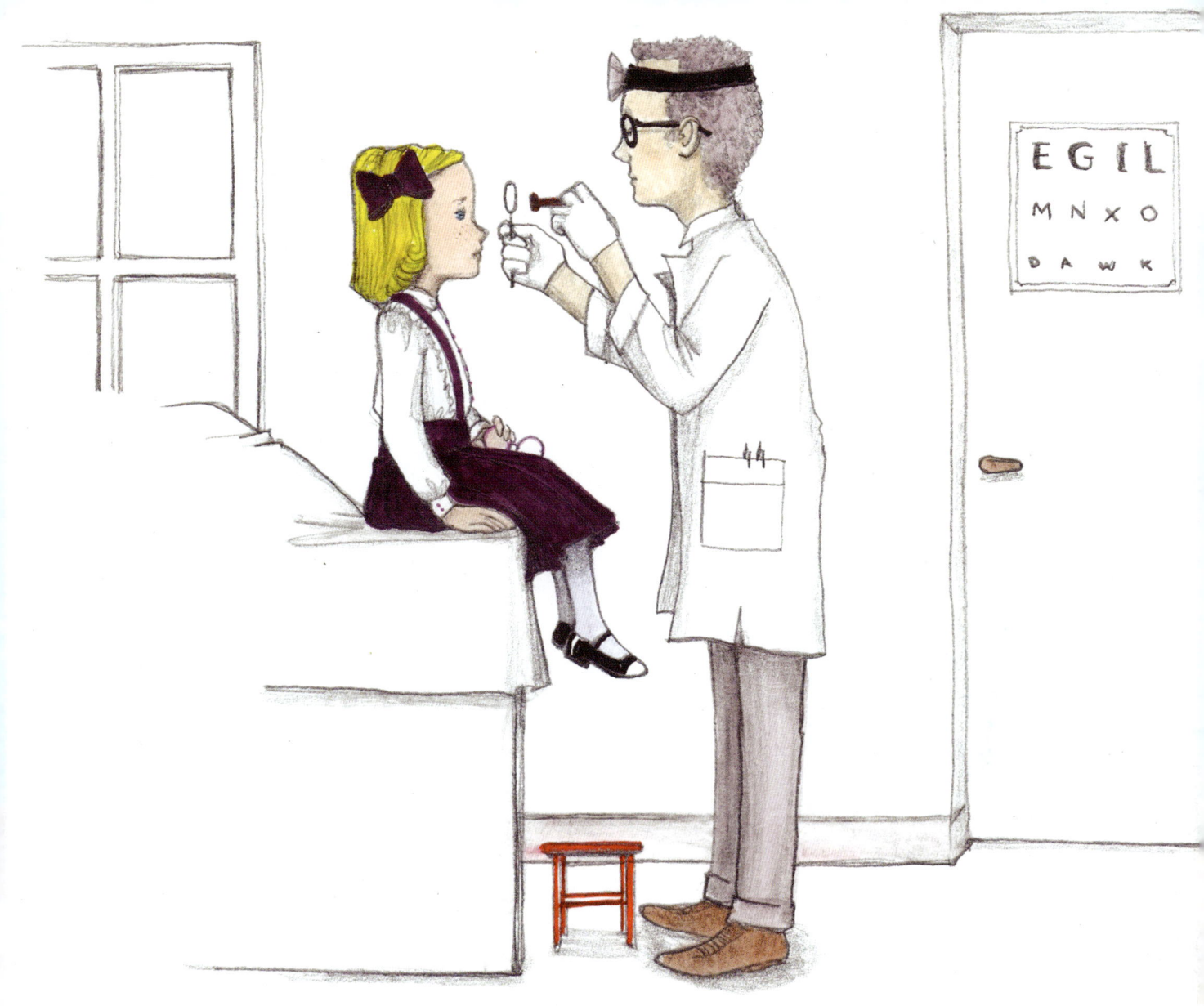

Dr. King asked me questions. Did my eyes sting? Were they watery? Did bright lights make them hurt?

I pointed to my left eye. "This one hurts," I said. "I just can't see through the fog."

Then Dr. King put drops in my eyes. He had me sit in the waiting room while he talked with my parents.

Soon the nurse led me back to Dr. King. He spent some time flashing bright lights in my eyes.

"Am I going to have to go to the hospital?" I asked. I'd had an operation on my right eye when I was little. It hadn't helped much. I still couldn't see very well with that eye.

"I don't think so, Val," the doctor said. "But I will have to check your eyes every few days." I thought he sounded worried. That made me worried too.

"Am I going to be blind, Dr. King?" I asked. I felt like crying.

A Cane in Her Hand 41

"We hope not, Val," he said slowly. "We're going to do all that we can to keep that from happening." Soon Mom was holding my hand. She said, "Dr. King wants us to talk to your teacher, Val. She can help you at school."

"She already does," I said. "She lets me go right up to the chalkboard to see stuff. She gives me books with large print to read. And special paper with black lines and a special pencil too. What else can Mrs. Johnson do?"

"We'll have to find out," my father said.

When Dr. King said it was okay, I went back to school. Mom went with me. She talked to Mrs. Johnson and other people.

It was a bad time. Lessons are hard when you can't see well. And I kept bumping into things, even when I tried my best to see what was in the way.

Then one Monday, Mrs. Johnson told me, "Miss Sousa is here. She's the special teacher for children who have trouble seeing. She helps with lessons. She'll also teach you how to travel by yourself so you won't get lost or hurt."

It sounded like it might be all right. But I hated to go to another room and leave my friends, even for a little while.

After Mrs. Johnson went back to the other kids, Miss Sousa gave me a test. She showed me some book pages. I read out loud those I could see.

Then we talked about how people who can't see well get around—by listening carefully, by touching, and by feeling with their hands and with their whole bodies sometimes. These were things I'd been doing for a long time without thinking about it.

I saw Miss Sousa two days a week after that. She helped me with schoolwork. She showed me how to hold my hands and arms so I wouldn't run smack into things I didn't see. I liked Miss Sousa. She's so nice you can't help liking her. I began to think going to her room wasn't so bad.

Then one day Miss Sousa held something out to me. It was a long cane.

"Oh, no!" I shouted. "I don't need that. Only blind people use canes. I'm not blind. I don't want it."

Miss Sousa didn't get mad. She said, "You know, Val, you're getting a lot of bumps lately. It's because you don't see some of the low things in your way. Your hands and arms don't reach far enough."

Well, that was true. It's no fun running into things. It hurts and it makes you feel stupid. I could use some help.

Miss Sousa put the cane in my hand. "A long cane is like a long arm," she said. "With it, you will find the low things before you bump into them."

"A long, skinny arm," I said, and Miss Sousa laughed.

She went on, "I've moved things around in here. I'm going to the other side of the room. I want you to follow me. Use your eyes and ears. Walk slowly. Use the cane as if it were your hand to find anything in your way."

I tried a few steps and moved the cane from side to side in front of me.

Ping! The cane hit the trash basket. I knew it was the trash basket by the sound it made. So I used the cane to find enough space to walk around it.

Plunk! A heavy chair. *Plink*! The leg of a metal table. I walked around everything.

"How about that!" Miss Sousa said. "You followed me across the room and didn't bump into anything." I felt sort of proud. But I didn't like the noise the cane made and the way it felt in my hand. Still, it was fun to guess what things were from the sounds they made.

"Do you know what you were doing?" Miss Sousa asked. "You were cane traveling. It's not easy. Let me show you how to use your cane so it won't be so noisy and clumsy."

In the next few weeks Miss Sousa taught me how to hold and use a long cane to travel indoors. I was glad we practiced in her room. It was easier with just the two of us. Each time, she put more things in my way. I learned to tell what was in my way by the sound it made and by how it felt when I touched it with the cane. Then I found how to go around it.

"Val," Miss Sousa said one day, "you're getting to be a very good cane traveler." She made it sound like being a good swimmer or skater. Then she said, "Let me know when you want to practice in the hall."

I wasn't sure I liked that idea. In the room it was okay, but maybe people in the hall wouldn't understand. How about my friends?

Well, they understood! It didn't make any difference to them. Miss Sousa had me practice going from my room to the gym and to the music room. I had my own cane now.

Later, I took my cane outdoors and learned how to find the edge of the walk or a hedge or a fence to help me stay on the path. Miss Sousa stayed right with me.

Now my long cane takes lots of bumps for me. I use it at school, especially going to different rooms. I take it with me when I go places. I don't often go to new places alone. But someday I will, and my cane will keep me from bumping into things or falling when I come to a curb.

Do I mind not being able to see as well as other kids? Yes, I do. But what I mind most is having people talk about me as if I'm not there.

One day I went to the store for Mom. Mrs. Wong, who owns the store, was talking to a woman whose voice I didn't know.

The woman saw my cane and said, "She's such a pretty girl. Too bad she can't see."

That hurt! It made me mad too. Didn't she think I could hear her? Or did she think I was too stupid to understand?

Mrs. Wong understood. It made her mad too. She knows there are lots of things a kid can do without being able to see very well. She knows I can do most things kids in my neighborhood do.

I roller-skate. (Maybe I fall down sometimes, but so does everybody.) I swim. (At camp I won a medal for swimming.) I paint pictures and make things out of clay. I am learning to play the organ. I take dancing lessons.

I have learned to do many things. And like other kids, I'm going to learn a lot more. Miss

Sousa says the most important thing I'm learning is to think for myself.

I wish other people would learn that too. Then they'd know there are lots of ways of seeing. Seeing with your eyes is important, but it isn't everything.

About the Author

Ada B. Litchfield was born in 1916 in Harwich, Massachusetts. She worked as an elementary school teacher, editor, and writer of children's books. Mrs. Litchfield wrote 13 children's books, many of them about science or about people with disabilities.

I Go Forth to Move About the Earth

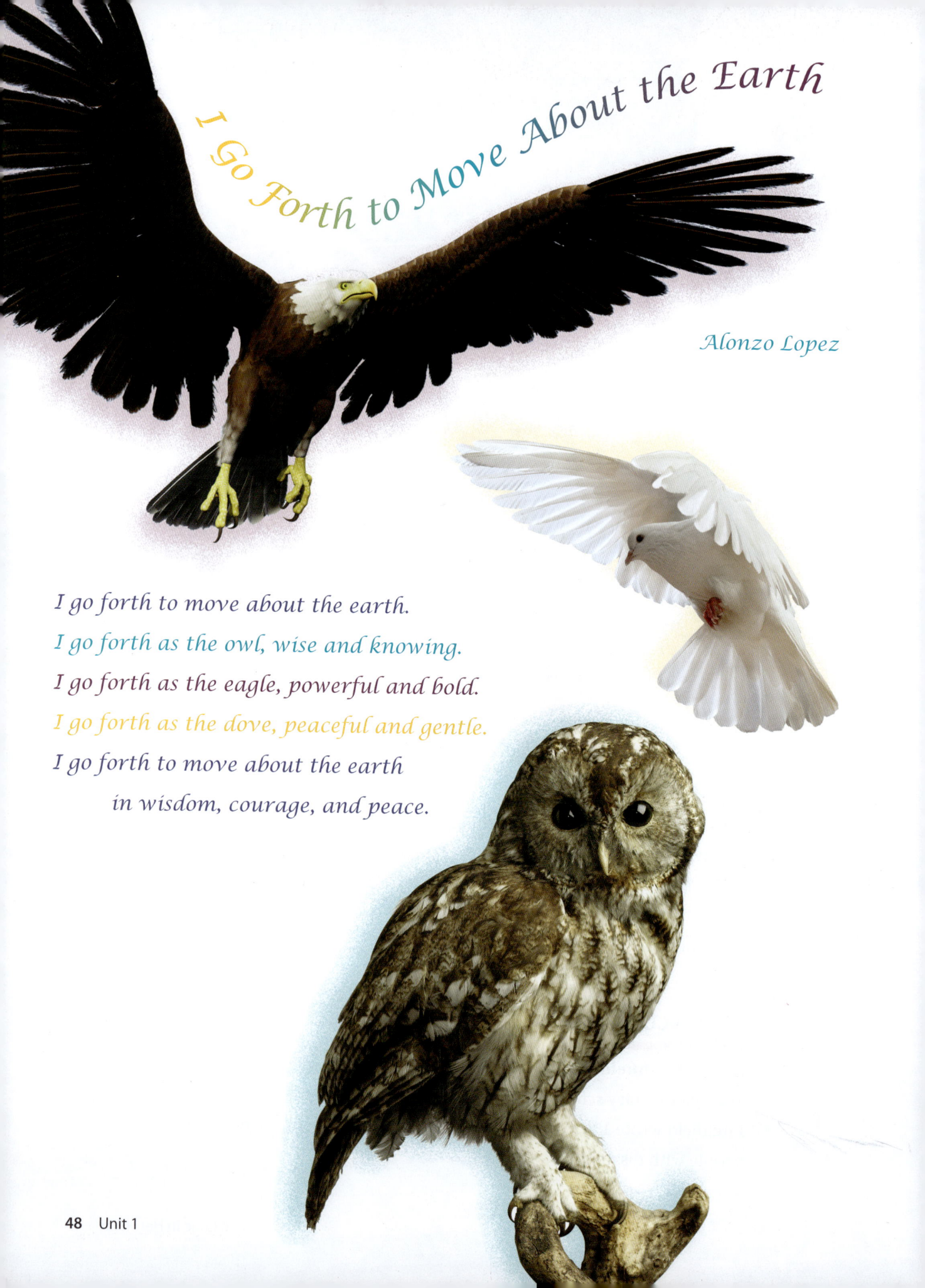

Alonzo Lopez

I go forth to move about the earth.
I go forth as the owl, wise and knowing.
I go forth as the eagle, powerful and bold.
I go forth as the dove, peaceful and gentle.
I go forth to move about the earth
   in wisdom, courage, and peace.

Studying the Selection

FIRST IMPRESSIONS
Why do you think Valerie became so successful at making friends and at activities like swimming, painting, and dancing?

QUICK REVIEW
1. When did Valerie first notice she was seeing things through a fog?
2. What was Miss Sousa's job?
3. What did Valerie say when Miss Sousa offered her a cane?
4. What are four things that Valerie can do just like other kids?

FOCUS
5. What was the most important lesson Miss Sousa taught Valerie?
6. Although this story is mainly about Valerie, it is also about Miss Sousa, Valerie's parents, the doctor, and Valerie's friends. Choose one of these characters and write about three qualities that this character has. For example, you could write that the doctor is friendly, serious, and helpful.

CREATING AND WRITING
7. One day, a lady in Mrs. Wong's store said something that hurt and angered Valerie. Look back at the story and see what that was. Now, imagine that you are Mrs. Wong and that Valerie has just left the store. You want to explain to the lady what she did wrong. Write a paragraph in which you respectfully explain to the lady why her words were hurtful.
8. Vision is not something to take for granted. It is a precious gift that we must guard. Your teacher will divide the class into groups and distribute poster board and markers. Each group will make a sign about protecting their eyesight. The sign should include a list of three rules to follow for strong, healthy eyes and a picture that illustrates each rule.

Lesson in Literature...
LIFE ON MARS

WHAT IS SETTING?
- The *time* and *place* in which the story's events happen are the story's **setting**.
- The *time* includes the time of day and the season of the year. It might include the year in which the story takes place.
- The *place* includes the country, the city, and even the building in which the story happens.
- When you read a story, think of it as a play you are watching. Imagine the scenery that would be on the stage—that is the story's setting.

THINK ABOUT IT!
1. What is the setting of *Life on Mars*? Make sure you include both time and place.
2. What are three ways that Mars is different from Earth?
3. What did you think was going to happen when Jon tasted the bubbling mixture?

The first people who came to Mars were astronauts. After them, regular explorers who walked around and made maps came. Next, people from big corporations like electric companies came. They were going to pay for the colony.

The second round of visitors was mostly scientists. They looked closely at rocks, the rust-colored sand, and the polar icecaps. The scientists wanted to see if human beings could live on Mars. What would colonists do on Mars for food and air?

Mars has no atmosphere. This means nothing holds in the oxygen that we breathe. Also, nothing traps the heat from the sun so it is very cold here. The only way human beings could live on Mars is in a dome, a very high and long and wide plastic dome filled with oxygen. To go outside, people must wear spacesuits. Spacesuits provide oxygen and warmth.

My family and I arrived on Mars in 2275. We were Moonies. My sisters and I were born on the Moon. Only my Mom and Dad had been to Earth. They went back home to be trained as food scientists. On Mars, they would ensure that what people ate was safe. They would try to invent new recipes from chemicals, and also from food grown in the fake soil under special lights within the dome.

I was ten when we came here. I hadn't expected Mars to be so beautiful. Outside the dome there is a haze that looks like cinnamon. If you live on Earth you might find it strange here because the mountains are tiny, Mars is only half the size of Earth, and it has *two* moons.

I like Mars, but sometimes I am bored. Even though we have a huge gym, I feel I never get enough exercise. We can't just run around. My sisters and I also complain about the food. There isn't much variety. When my birthday was coming, I thought, *Just one more birthday with no ice cream*! I was going to be thirteen.

It was 2278. My parents' laboratory had grown to include several rooms. They had several assistants. The experiments always looked interesting. My sisters and I would go there when we finished our studies.

Some of the experiments looked like ordinary liquids in glass beakers. The ones that could be tasted were marked with a Y for YES. We liked tasting the liquids and leaving our comments. But I wanted to show my parents that I could be a chemist, too.

I know it was wrong of me. But I wanted to see what would happen if we combined small amounts from two or three separate beakers. There were several liquids that tasted sweet, but they were too watery. So in a separate container, I added thick, almost creamy, goo. This made it sweeter and thicker, but way too sticky.

My younger sister, Bess, said, "Well, how about this one? It is shiny and smooth!"

Caroline, the older of the two, said excitedly, "Yeah! Let's try that!" So we added it to the mix.

There were lots of bubbles, and then some hissing and sizzle. Steam rose from the beaker.

The two girls shouted, "Taste it, Jon. It's *your* experiment!"

I took a tablespoon and helped myself. Ice cream. Plain and simple. Ice cream for birthdays and celebrations. Ice cream we could sell at a stand.

Now we just had to remember how we had made it.

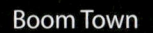

Blueprint for Reading

INTO . . . *Boom Town*

Amanda was a can-do person. When something was needed, she tried to help, and where Amanda lived, *everything* was needed! Out in California in the Gold Rush days, people lived in lonely places that had not much more than a water pump. Except for the few people who found gold, everyone was poor. Amanda, just a young girl, decided to cheer up her family with homemade pies. Then Pa began to sell slices of Amanda's pie, and a business was born. But what about the neighbors? Could Amanda help them?

EYES ON *Setting*

The **setting** is *where* and *when* a story takes place. *Where* might be the African jungle, a busy street in New York, or a space station on Mars. *When* could be 200 years ago or right now or some time in the future. When we read, we use our imaginations. We see the story's setting in our minds. This is called "using our mind's eye." When you read *Boom Town*, imagine a town with rough log cabins, dirt paths, and not much else. Use your mind's eye to picture the town as it changes, and changes, and changes!

BOOM TOWN

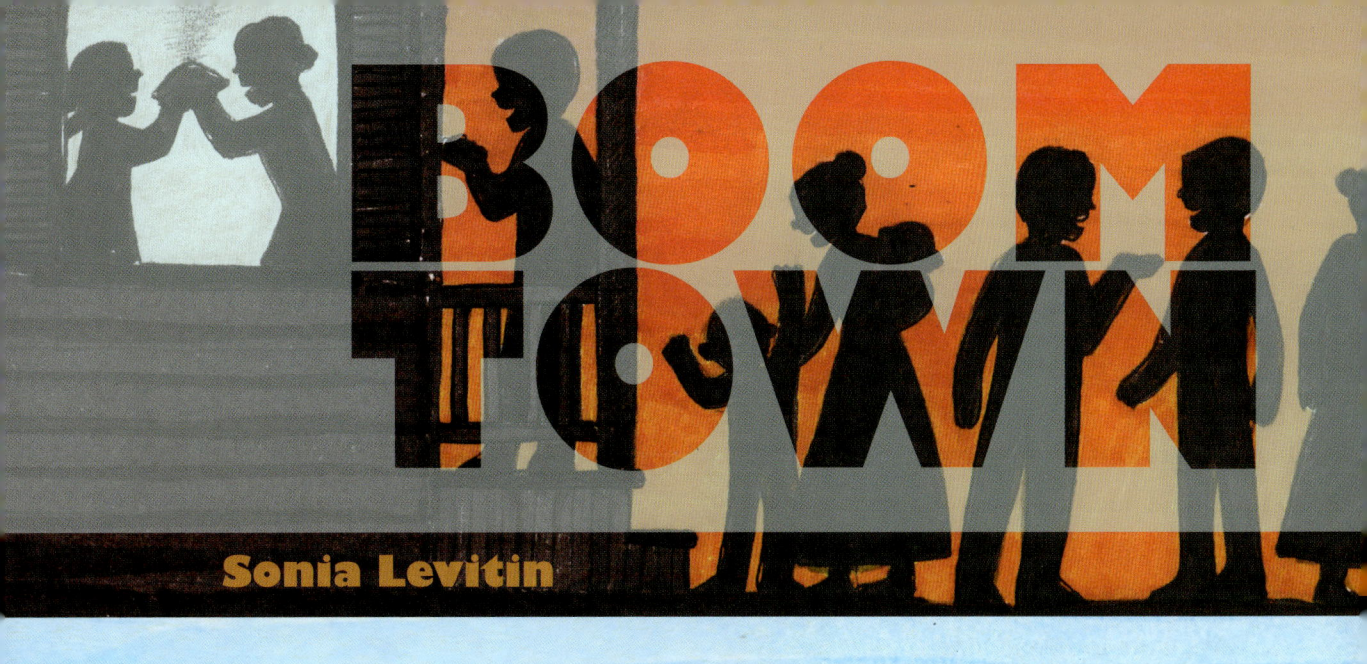

Sonia Levitin

It took us twenty-one days on the stagecoach to get to California. When we got there, I thought we'd live with Pa in the gold fields. A whole tent city was built up. But Ma shook her head. "The gold fields are no place for children. We'll get a cabin and live in town."

What town? A stage stop, a pump house, a few log cabins—that was all. It was so wide and lonesome out west, even my shadow ran off.

Ma found a cabin big enough for all of us: Baby Betsy, brothers Billy, Joe, Ted, and me—Amanda. Pa came in from the gold fields every Saturday night, singing:

"So I got me a mule
And some mining tools,
A shovel and a pick and a pan;
But I work all day
Without no pay.
I guess I'm a foolish man."

> **WORD BANK**
> **stagecoach** *n*.: a horse-drawn coach that carried passengers, mail, and packages

Boom Town 53

First Ma made him take a bath in a tin tub set out under the stars. Then Pa sang songs and told stories he'd heard from the miners—stories about men finding big nuggets and striking it rich. But poor Pa, he had no luck at all. Still, every Monday morning he'd leave for the gold fields full of hope.

Days were long and lonely. The hills spread out as far as forever. Nights, me and Ma and my brothers and Baby Betsy would sit out and wait for a shooting star to sail across the sky. Once in a while a crow flew by. That's all the excitement there was.

My brothers worked up some furrows. They planted corn and potatoes and beans. Then they ran around climbing trees, skinning their knees. But after all the water was fetched and the wash was done, after the soap was made and the fire laid, after the beds were fixed and the floor was swept clean, I'd sit outside our cabin door with Baby Betsy, so bored I thought I'd die. Also, I hankered for some pie. I loved to bake pie.

Word Bank

furrows *n.*: narrow grooves made in the ground

I asked Ma and she said, "Pie would be good, but we have no pie pans and no real oven, just the wood stove. How would you bake pie?"

I poked around in a big box of stuff and found an old iron skillet. I decided to make a pie crust and pick gooseberries to fill it.

Gooseberries grew on the bushes near town. I picked a big pailful and went back home. I made a crust with flour, butter, a little water, and a pinch of salt, and then I rolled it out.

Ma came in and said, "Looks good, Amanda. I knew you could make it. But tell me, how will you bake it?"

I showed Ma the skillet. She shook her head. "I don't think it will work, but you can try."

"It will work," I said.

WORD BANK

skillet *n.*: frying pan

Brothers Billy and Joe and Ted stood there laughing. When the wood turned to coals, I pushed my pie inside the old stove. After a while I smelled a bad burning. I pulled out my pie, hard as a rock. Billy, Joe, and Ted whooped and slapped their sides. They snatched up my pie and tossed it high into the air. They ran outside and Billy whacked it hard with a stick. Pie pieces flew all over the place, and my brothers bent over, laughing.

I was so mad I went right back in to make another, and I promised none of them would get a bite. I rolled out my crust and filled it with berries, shoved the pie into the oven and soon took it out.

I set the pie down to cool. I went off to do some mending. Next thing I knew, Baby Betsy, just learning to walk, sat there with pie goo all over her face. Too soft, the filling ran down on Betsy, and she wailed like a coyote in the night.

It took one more try, but I got it right. That night we ate my gooseberry pie, and it was delicious.

When Pa came home from the gold fields on Saturday night, there was a pie for him, too. "Amanda, you are the queen of the kitchen!" Pa scooped me up and whirled me around. I was proud.

The next week I made an extra pie for Pa to take with him to the gold fields.

Saturday night when he came home singing, coins jangled in his pocket.

We all ran out to ask, "Did you strike gold, Pa?"

"No," he said. "I sold Amanda's pie. The miners loved it. They paid me twenty-five cents a slice!"

After that, Pa took pies to the gold fields every week. And every week he came home with coins in his pockets. Some miners walked right to our door looking for pie. They told Ma, "You should open a bakery."

Ma said, "It's my girl Amanda who is the baker. If she wants to make pies, that's fine. But I have no time."

Ma had a new baby on the way. It was up to me. I figured I could sell pies to the miners and fill up our money jar.

Boom Town 57

But I needed help. I rounded up my brothers and told them, "If you want to eat pie, you've got to work."

They grumbled and groaned, but they knew I meant it. So Billy built me a shelf, Joe made a sign, AMANDA'S FINE PIES, and Ted helped pick berries and sour apples.

I needed more pans and another bucket. One day Peddler Pete came by, and with the money I'd made I bought them.

"You're a right smart little girl," said the peddler, "being in business like this."

I thought fast and told him, "Anybody can make money out here. Folks need things all the time, and there're no stores around. If you were to settle and start one, I'll bet you'd get rich."

Peddler Pete scratched his beard. "Not a bad idea," he said. "My feet are sore from roaming. I could use this cart and build my way up to having a store."

So pretty soon we had us a real store called PEDDLER PETE'S TRADING POST. Trappers and traders and travelers appeared. After shopping at Pete's, they were good and hungry.

They came to our cabin, looking for pie. Some liked it here so well they decided to stay. Soon we had a cooper, a tanner, a miller, a blacksmith. A town was starting to grow.

Word Bank

cooper *n.*: a person who makes or repairs barrels or tubs

tanner *n.*: a person who makes leather out of animal hides

miller *n.*: a person who grinds grain into flour

blacksmith *n.*: a person who makes horseshoes and puts them on the horses

A prospector came in on the stage from St. Joe, his clothes covered with dirt. He looked around at the folks eating pie, and he asked, "Is there someone here who does washing?"

I stepped right up and I told him, "What we need is a laundry. Why don't you stay and start one? Why, the miners are sending their shirts clear to China. You'll make more money doing laundry than looking for gold."

The man thought a while, then said with a smile, "You're right, little lady. It's a dandy idea. I'll send for my wife to help."

Soon shirts and sheets fluttered on the line as people brought their washing in. A tailor came to make and mend clothes. A cobbler crafted shoes and boots. We heard the *tap tap* of his hammer and smelled the sweet leather. A barber moved in with shaving mugs, and an apothecary with herbs and healing drugs. So the town grew up all around us.

> **WORD BANK**
>
> **prospector** (PROSS pek ter) *n.*: a person who searches and digs for gold in certain areas
>
> **apothecary** (uh PAH thuh keh ree) *n.*: a pharmacy

My pie business blossomed. Sometimes the line snaked clear around the house. Baby Betsy entertained the people while they waited. Billy added another shelf. Joe and Ted made a bench. We all picked berries and apples. Even Ma came to help. We had to get a bigger jar for all the money coming in.

One day our old friend Cowboy Charlie rode by. Like everyone else, he stopped for some pie. "I'd like to rest a spell," he said. "Where can I leave my horse for the night?"

Word Bank

blossomed (BLAH sumd) *v.*: grew and developed tremendously

Boom Town 61

"There's no livery stable," I said. "But why don't you start one? You'd rent out horses, and wagons too. That would be the perfect business for you."

"You're just full of great ideas, little lady," Cowboy Charlie said. He twirled his lariat. "I'd like to settle down. I'll stay here and do just that."

Soon a trail was worn right to Charlie's stable door. All day we heard the snorting of horses. Now Charlie needed hay. Farmers brought wagons and sacks full of feed. With all those people riding in, someone decided to build a hotel and a cafe. The town grew fast all around us.

The owner of the cafe bought pies from me, five or six at a time. I taught Billy how to roll the crust. Joe got wood for the stove. Ted washed the fruit, and Baby Betsy tried to stir in the sugar.

> **WORD BANK**
>
> **livery** (LIH vuh ree) *n.*: a place where horses are cared for, fed, and stabled for pay
>
> **lariat** (LARE ee ut) *n.*: lasso; a long, noosed rope used to catch horses, cattle, or other livestock

The money jar in our kitchen looked ready to bust. Where could we safely keep all that cash? Lucky us, one day Mr. Hooper, the banker, appeared.

"I'm building a bank," Mr. Hooper said to me. "This is getting to be a boom town."

"We'll use your bank," I told Mr. Hooper, "but the roads are so poor. In winter there's mud, and in summer there's dust. We need some sidewalks and better streets."

"You're a smart little lady," said Mr. Hooper, tipping his hat. "I'll see what I can do about that."

Before we knew it, the bank was built and wooden sidewalks were laid. One street was called Bank Street; the other was Main. Soon every lane and landmark had a name. Pa and my brothers built on a big room for our bakery.

Men sent for their families. New houses appeared everywhere. Babies and children filled up the town. We needed a school, and a good schoolmarm.

We knew Miss Camilla from our stagecoach days. She was living up the coast a ways. Cowboy Charlie rode off to fetch her, and she was glad to come.

Miss Camilla, the teacher, had married, and her husband came too. We all got together to build a school. Bells rang out every day of the week. Now this was a real boom town!

One day Pa said to me, "Amanda, I'm through panning for gold. Will you let me be in business with you?"

"Sure!" I said, happily. "I'd love to work with you, Pa, and I'd also like to go to school."

So Pa turned to baking, and we all worked together. Pa sang while he rolled out the dough:

"Amanda found a skillet
And berries to fill it,
Made pies without a pan;

Our pies are the best
In all the West.
I guess I'm a lucky man."

Now Pa is with us every day. There's excitement and bustle all around. Our house sits in the middle of a boom town! And to think it all started with me, Amanda, baking pies!

ABOUT THE AUTHOR

Born in Berlin, Germany, **Sonia Levitin** and her family came to America when Sonia was four years old. She grew up riding horses, feeding stray cats, climbing trees, and, of course, reading and writing. When she was eleven years old, she wrote a letter to author Laura Ingalls Wilder telling her that she wanted to become a writer. Mrs. Levitin has taught both children and adults, and her books for children and young adults have won many awards. Her goal in writing is to connect people. She says writing "must flow, laugh, sing, and dance with you."

GENERAL STORE

Rachel Field

Someday I'm going to have a store
With a tinkly bell hung over the door,
With real glass cases and counters wide
And drawers all spilly with things inside.
There'll be a little of everything:
Bolts of calico; balls of string;
Jars of peppermint; tins of tea;
Pots and kettles and crockery;
Seeds in packets; scissors bright;
Kegs of sugar, brown and white;
Sarsaparilla for picnic lunches,
Bananas and rubber boots in bunches.
I'll fix the window and dust each shelf,
And take the money in all myself,
It will be my store and I will say:
"What can I do for you to-day?"

Studying the Selection

FIRST IMPRESSIONS
Can one person really make a difference?

QUICK REVIEW

1. Why had Amanda's family come to California?
2. After weeks of coming home with nothing at all, how did Pa manage to finally bring home a little money?
3. What were some of the businesses that sprung up in the town?
4. What did Pa finally decide to do instead of looking for gold?

FOCUS

5. Amanda was full of ideas and suggestions. How did she know what to suggest to the different people she met?
6. The setting of a story includes the time and place in which the story happens. Imagine that you are Amanda and you have just arrived in the little town. You are taking a walk around. Write at least three sentences describing what you see.

CREATING AND WRITING

7. Amanda built up a business by starting small. First she baked one pie for her family. By the end of the story, her family is running a bakery for an entire town. Can you think of a business that might have started very small? If you know of one, write a paragraph describing how it started and what it grew into. If you don't know of one, you may invent one and write about it.
8. This story describes a lot of old-fashioned businesses, like cobblers, tanners, millers, and blacksmiths. On a sheet of paper, make a small ad for one of those businesses, or others that might have been built in a boom town. Make sure you include the name of your business, its address (make one up), and maybe a sentence describing how good your business is. You may even draw a small picture or logo. Your teacher will collect the sheets of paper and put them together to form a Yellow Pages of all the businesses in town.

Boom Town 67

Jill's Journal:
On Assignment in Rhyolite, Nevada

Hi. My name is Jill. I'm a reporter. I go places so I can tell my readers the story about what I see. Sometimes, as with this assignment, it means I have to go back in time.

I am interested in boom towns, how people come and then they go. Old boom towns of the West grew up around mines. They began as little camps with tents. As people in the East or in other countries heard about a new mine—especially a gold mine—more and more people came. They thought they would make lots of money from finding precious metal.

After a while, a general store and other shops would open. There would be a blacksmith to make shoes for horses and a wheelwright to fix wagon wheels. Newcomers also opened restaurants, boarding houses, and hotels. When whole families came, they would build cabins. In many boom towns, most buildings were put up so quickly that they were not sturdy or safe.

Boom towns were not very well-organized. There was no running water, no streetlights, no paved sidewalks, and no rules. Trash was piled up in back of the buildings. Because of this, boom towns were smelly and dirty. Also, they were very noisy. When men returned from the mine at night, there was shouting and there were fights. Sometimes there were gunfights and people got badly hurt.

Boarding houses and hotels were usually small. Hotels were often on the second floor of the restaurants. The general store was a place where people gathered during the day and exchanged news. The merchants who ran the stores, the hotels, and the restaurants made more money selling goods and services to the miners than most of the miners made trying to find gold.

A mine would be worked until it had no more precious metal to mine. No one knew when that would be. But when it occurred, there might be no reason to stay in the town. Many boom towns became deserted.

This is why I am interested in boom towns: One day there are lots of people in the town, and the next day everyone may leave and it becomes a ghost town. *Ghost town* sounds a little scary and very mysterious to me.

Therefore, I have decided to go to the boom town called Rhyolite. Rhyolite is in southwestern Nevada and has an interesting history. By the way, it may be hard to believe, but it is 1908. I went from Los Angeles by train. At Las Vegas I boarded another rail for the 118-mile trip to Rhyolite. This train has only three passenger cars! We have been traveling for five hours. The trip takes six, but I am lucky to have Mrs. Edna Montgomery sitting next to me. She knows I am a reporter from back East, so she is filling me in. I believe she, herself, is a bit of a historian.

Edna has told me that in this part of Nevada, there are several boom towns. She says that in 1904, two men found gold in a hill they called Bullfrog Mountain. This gold was worth a lot of money. As word of their discovery spread, thousands of people came to the region looking for gold.

Now, she says, 5,000 people live in Rhyolite. As we pull into the train depot, I gasp in surprise, "This train station is so beautiful!"

Edna says, "It should be. Why, Mr. Schwab spent $130,000 on it!"

She pats my arm and says proudly, "Jill, there are 19 lodging houses, 24 restaurants, 6 barbers, a public bathhouse, and a daily newspaper in Rhyolite. You may want to take a peek at the new bonnets at Molly's, as well. But I have to be on my way. My husband and children are waiting inside the depot. Why don't you take a walk over to the offices of the *Rhyolite Herald*, our newspaper, and meet one of your fellow reporters? When

Jill's Journal

Cook Bank Building — 1908 / 2009

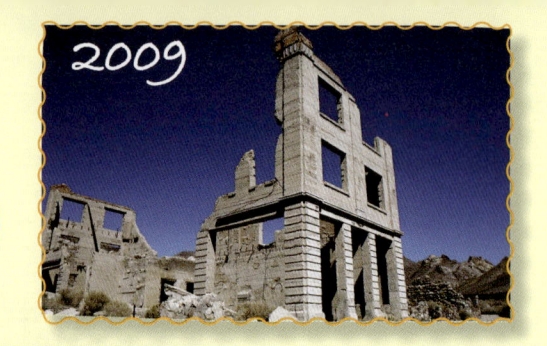

you've finished looking around town, please join us for tea." This nice woman gives me her address and we part.

As I begin to walk about, I see that Rhyolite is nothing like the usual dirty and muddy boom towns. A very wealthy man whom Edna mentioned, Charles Schwab, bought the mine and spent lots of money here. He had water piped in, paid for an electric line that had to run 100 miles to get to Rhyolite, and even had a train line run to the mine.

I cannot believe it, but right now I am walking on a concrete sidewalk. This place was just desert four years ago. There are electric lights and telephone and telegraph lines! I pass the police and fire departments. Edna said that unlike other boom towns, Rhyolite has laws. I pass a hospital. I am amazed. I wish you could see the Cook Bank Building. It is actually three stories high!

Now I have come to the school. The school has two stories and eight rooms! It is full of children studying and playing. The school also makes room for adults who want to learn how to read and write.

I have walked for several hours and my feet hurt. I stop a passerby and ask for directions to Edna Montgomery's house. The gentleman is dressed like a miner and covered with dust, but he is very helpful. He exclaims, "Ain't this a beautiful town?"

I smile in agreement. When I reach the Montgomerys' house, Edna welcomes me into the cool dining room. She asks me how my sightseeing went.

"I have enjoyed myself," I sigh. "I have been amazed by how busy this town is. Why, it is like a little city."

Edna introduces me to her children, four young ladies that range in age from seven to fifteen. The oldest girl, Dorothy, brings out a plate of muffins. Edna pours the tea into fine china cups that sit on matching saucers.

Two Story Schoolhouse — 1908 / 2009

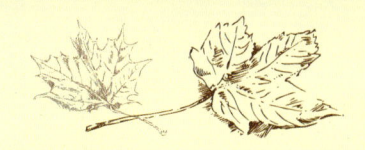

I think to myself, sadly, that in just two years, in 1910, the mines will dry up. I know this because I have come from many years in the future. Edna and her family do not know this, of course, and I cannot tell them. In 1910, there will be only 675 residents remaining. All the families will have moved away.

All the stores and restaurants will have closed. The banks will shut down. The newspapers, including the *Rhyolite Herald*, will be gone by June 1912. The post office will close in November 1913. The last train will leave Rhyolite Station in July 1914. Since there will be no people left, the Nevada-California Power Company will turn off the electricity and remove its lines in 1916.

After all, by 1916, Rhyolite, Nevada will be a ghost town.

POWER SKILL:
Organizing a Boom Town

1. You are going to compare the usual boom town with Rhyolite. We have given you some hints.

Usual Boom Town	Rhyolite
No rules	
	Well-constructed buildings
No sidewalks	
	A hospital
	Electricity
Dirty with garbage piled up	

2. What would you have done in a boom town? What supplies would you have needed to do this? Choose your business and make a list of what you need. Here are some choices. (You may also come up with your own ideas.)

General Store   **Doctor**
Pharmacy   **Teacher**
Restaurant   **Blacksmith**
Newspaper   **Wheelwright**

3. Make a sign for your business.

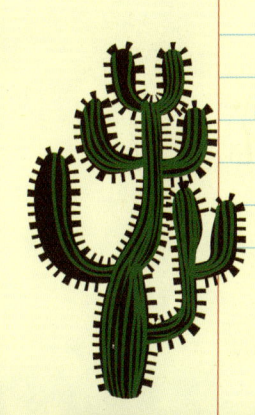

Jill's Journal 71

Lesson in Literature...
THE BLUE MARBLE

WHAT IS THEME?

- The **theme** of a story is its main idea.
- Sometimes, the author tells the reader exactly what the theme is. The author may state the theme right at the beginning of the story, somewhere in the middle, or all the way at the end.
- Other times, the reader must figure out what the theme is by thinking about the story. When that is the case, the theme will probably not be completely clear until the end of the story.
- All of the story elements—the plot, the characters, and the setting—help build the story's theme.

THINK ABOUT IT!

1. In this story, the author does not tell us what the theme is. However, the theme becomes clear at the very end of the story. Look at the last paragraph of the story and write down the story's theme.
2. In the story, Celi's father says something after a storm destroys their house. What does he say that hints at the theme?
3. The author tells us how Celi feels when she sees Maria's beautiful dress. What are those feelings? How do they hint at the theme?

Nicaragua is a country in Central America. There is a small town in Nicaragua called Bluefields. This is where Celi and Luci and Ada live. The three of them are good friends. They help each other with chores and with taking care of the babies in their families.

There is no road into Bluefields. Visitors either fly in or take a boat from the town of El Rama. Most of the people who live in Bluefields are very poor, but it is very beautiful there. There are 698 fabulous species of birds. The rain forest surrounds the town, except where the River Escondido flows.

Even though they are very poor, the three girls are usually very cheerful. Nicaragua has been badly hurt by hurricanes several times. When Hurricane Mitch came, heavy rains destroyed nearly 24,000 houses and 340 schools. When bad weather comes, Celi's father says, "It can't be helped. We just have to start over again. We are strong people and we will do just fine. We have to be happy with what we have."

Celi thinks her father is very brave. He is a fisherman and goes out every night in his boat. Her mother is a farmer. Her father has had to rebuild their house two times. She thinks maybe he should be a carpenter.

If they have time to play, the girls and their friends play marbles. A tourist once came to the town on a panga (which is a kind of boat). Before he left, he handed out about 200 marbles to the children. That is when the marble craze started. The children of the town never ask the tourists for anything except marbles.

The girls have no school today. They decide to play a game of marbles with a few friends. One girl, Maria, is wearing her beautiful Sunday dress. Her family has more than the other families. Celi tries hard not to be jealous. She doesn't have a special dress, just a clean old one her mother washed and ironed.

They all sit down on the hard-packed earth in a circle. Maria takes some new marbles out of her little marble pouch.

"Maria, where did you get those?" some of the girls cry. Maria empties the pouch onto a square of cloth. Celi sees a blue one. It looks like it glows. Maria pours out so many new marbles, she doesn't see that the blue one rolls away. Celi does not say anything. She knows that the blue marble is in the bushes.

Celi stands up, holding her marble bag tightly in her fist. "I'm sorry," she says. "I just remembered I said I would help my mother this afternoon. I can't play right now." She runs towards home.

Celi helps her mother, but all she can think about is the blue marble. She wants it so much. Surely Maria will not miss it. She has so many.

It is early evening. Celi is pretty sure the other girls have gone home. She runs back to the place where they were sitting in a circle. She walks over to the bushes. She crouches down. There is the marble, glowing like a little moon. Oh, how pretty it is!

Celi reaches for it and pricks her finger on a thorn. Her eyes fill with tears. She is about to do a very bad thing. She has never taken something that belonged to someone else. How can she need something so much that she would steal? She feels ashamed. She should be happy with what she has. She grabs the marble and runs to Maria's house.

Taro and the Tofu 73

Blueprint for Reading

INTO . . . *Taro and the Tofu*

Do you know what a *conscience* is? It is the part of you that reminds you to be a good person. Sometimes, we want to do the wrong thing, and then there is a little battle in our minds. One voice says, "It's all right to do that, it's not so bad." Another voice, our conscience, says, "No! Don't do that! It *is* wrong, and not at all like you!" In *Taro and the Tofu*, Taro, a boy about your age, is faced with a choice between right and wrong. As his two "little voices" argue, ask yourself: If I were Taro, what choice would *I* make?

EYES ON *Theme*

As we read through a story, we begin to see its main idea, called its **theme**. How can we tell which idea is the main one? Start by asking questions about the plot and characters. For example, when the little voice in Taro's head tells him to wait until the next day to return the money, we begin to think. We wonder why the little voice is telling him that. We wonder whether our own little voices would tell us the same thing. We wonder what Taro will answer the little voice. As we read and wonder, we begin to understand the idea that is growing in the story. We are discovering its theme.

Taro and the Tofu

Masako Matsuno

It was windy, and the wind was cold. The cold, windy day was growing into a cold, windy night. From the window Taro could see the evening star already shining brightly in the east. Taro was watching for the tofu seller.

In Japan *tofu* is what we call "bean curd"—it is very delicious, and it is one of the most important foods of that country.

Taro's mother bought tofu from a man who came along the street every evening. But on this cold, windy evening, the man did not come.

In their warm house Taro and his mother waited and waited until finally it was time to cook supper.

"I wonder what has happened to him," said Taro's mother. "This is the first time he hasn't come without letting us know."

"Shall I run to his shop?" asked Taro.

His mother was unsure. "It's getting dark … and cold, too."

"That's all right," said Taro, "it's not so late yet, is it? I'll get the tofu for you, Mother."

From beyond the woods the cold wind blew. Taro, holding a small pan for tofu in one hand and a silver coin in the other, began running as soon as he left the house.

The shopping street was crowded with people buying good food for supper. The shops were light and cheerful.

"Come in and buy, come in and buy! My fish are delicious!" a loud voice called from one of the fish stores.

But Taro didn't stop—this wasn't the place he was looking for. He ran in the direction of the man's shop which was at the end of the street, away from the main shopping place. That was why he went to the houses every evening to sell tofu.

Taro and the Tofu 77

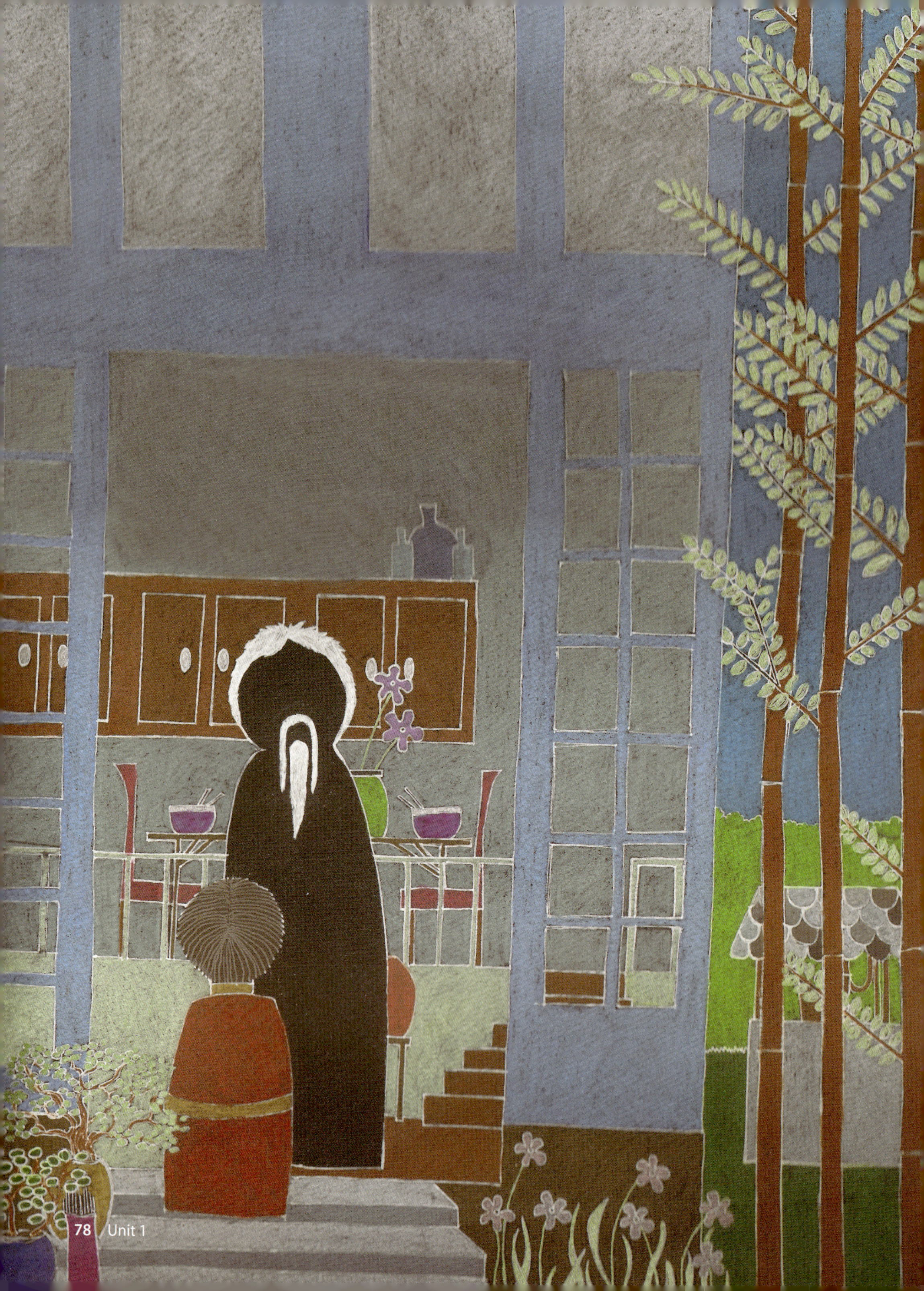

Taro hurried through the crowd. Beyond the lights and noise of the shops it was cold and dark and lonely; only one dim light showed at the very end of the street. It was the light of the man's shop.

The man was surprised to see Taro. "Are you alone?" he asked. "Did you come here all by yourself?"

"Yes," said Taro. "My mother needs two cakes of tofu. She waited a long time for you to come, but you didn't come. What happened?"

The man took the tofu pan from Taro and said, "I'm sorry, but my grandson doesn't feel well today, so I couldn't leave him alone. But I'll come to your house tomorrow evening," the man added. He handed Taro the filled tofu pan, saying, "Then you won't have to come down in the cold."

"How much?" asked Taro.

"Thirty yen."[1]

Taro handed the coin to the man, who slowly counted out the change under the dim light of the shop.

"Thank you, Taro," he said. "You'd better hurry home, for your mother must be waiting for you."

"Yes—good-by!"

"Don't run, Taro!" the man shouted after him. "My tofu is soft. Carry it carefully so it doesn't break!"

---

1. A *yen* is the smallest coin in Japan, similar to a U.S. penny.

Taro did not run, but he walked fast. Whenever Taro did an errand, his mother let him keep ten yen for himself, so he was in a hurry to get to the little candy store on the main shopping street.

The candy store was run by a lady with big glasses. She always sat in a far corner of the shop, reading a newspaper. She rarely said more than a few words to people. "Thank you, good boy," or "Thank you, good girl," she would say, never looking up from her paper. It was one of the seven wonders to Taro how she knew a boy was a boy—or a girl a girl—without ever looking at them.

And the lady never seemed to care if the children took a long time to decide what to buy with their pocket money. It made Taro feel that all the candies in the store belonged to him until at last he decided just what to buy.

Taro had to decide quickly today so he could hurry home with the tofu.

Two boxes of chocolate, he said to himself, putting his hand in his pocket for the change the man had given him. Taro picked one of the coins to give to the lady.

Taro and the Tofu   81

But, wait, it was a 50-yen coin!

Where did I get this?

Taro looked at the coin in surprise.

"I thought the man gave me seven 10-yen coins, for the tofu was thirty yen, and I gave him a 100-yen coin," thought Taro. "One, two, three, four, five, six … Here are six 10-yen coins and a 50-yen … Then the man made a mistake. I must return the extra forty yen to him right away. He will be sorry if he finds that he lost money."

But outside it was already dark and the wind was very cold.

"It's getting late, and very cold ..." a strange little voice whispered inside Taro's head. "Why not tomorrow? Even if the man worries, the mistake is his own fault. It's very cold, and Mother must be waiting," the secret voice said.

Taro looked at the money in his hand and then at the cold outdoors. "It's just the same if you give the money back tomorrow," whispered the voice again. "Besides, who knows that you've got the money? No one need know. Just think, with forty yen to spend, you could buy sweet beans and salted beans and chocolate and even more ... Right?"

"Oh, no—" it was almost a shout inside him—"No, no, it's not right. This is not my money. It belongs to the man, even if it was his fault that he gave me the wrong change. I don't want the candies!" Taro was talking to himself very fast now, as if he were in a hurry to rid himself of the strange, secret voice inside his head. "I will return the money right now."

Taro called to the lady of the candy store, but his voice sounded so dry and cracked that only a little low whisper came out.

"I'll take two boxes of chocolate candy today," he said.

"Thank you, good boy," answered the lady without looking up.

Taro smiled. "And may I leave my tofu pan here for just a little while?" he asked.

"Of course you may, good boy," answered the lady, still looking at her newspaper.

Taro put the tofu pan down carefully beside a 10-yen coin for the candies and ran out of the store. He ran down the cheerful shopping street, through the crowds of people; he was still running when he reached the little shop.

"Back so soon?" said the man, seeing Taro. "Does your mother need more tofu?"

"No—I came to give this money back to you," said Taro.

"What money?"

"You gave me the wrong change; you gave me forty extra yen."

"Really? I didn't even see it. Are you sure the money isn't yours?"

"Yes," said Taro, "I'm sure that you gave me a 50-yen coin for a 10-yen coin. I'll put the money here, all right? I must hurry because Mother is waiting for me."

"Thank you very much, Taro," said the man with gladness in his face.

Taro was happy, but he felt shy too, for he remembered the strange little voice.

"Not at all," he said quickly. Before he knew it he found himself taking one of the boxes of chocolate candy from his pocket. "For your grandson," he said.

"Thank you … thank you …"

Taro and the Tofu   85

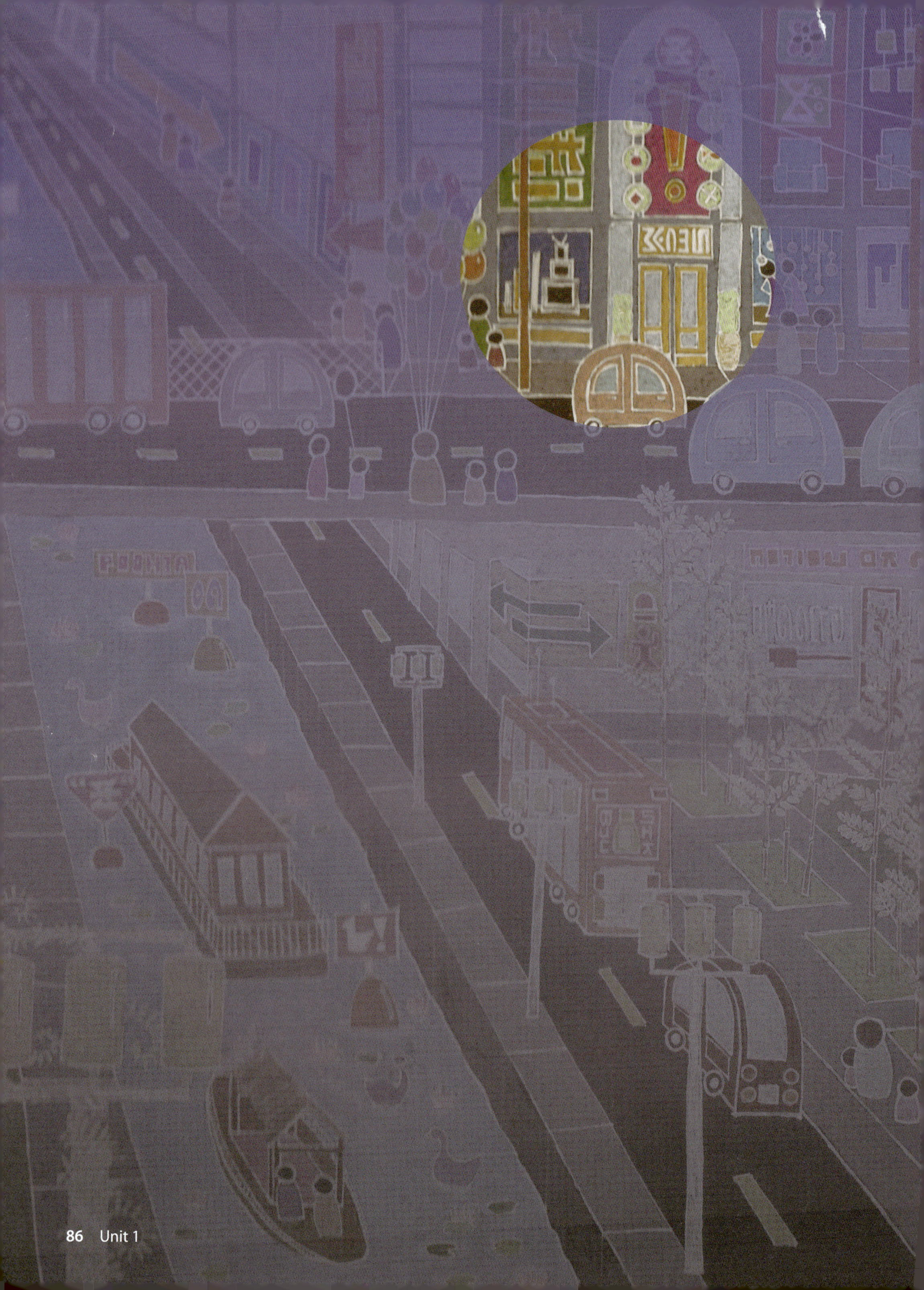

The lady in the candy store was still reading her newspaper when Taro stopped to pick up the tofu pan.

"Thank you for keeping it for me," said Taro.

"Not at all, good boy," said the lady, and much to Taro's surprise, she looked up, straight at him.

Taro had never seen her look at anything but her newspaper. What was more, she was smiling at him—it was almost as if she knew what had happened—but, no, it couldn't be!

"You'd better hurry, good boy. It's very late," said the lady.

Taro nodded and went out of the store with his tofu pan.

Most of the shops on the shopping street were closed now, and only a few people were still there. The wind was very cold.

Anyway, thought Taro, I don't really care if the lady knows what the voice said, because I gave back the money.

He was so happy that he wanted to run all the way home, but he remembered to walk carefully with the tofu. His hands ached with the cold by the time he got there.

At home Taro told his mother and father what had happened to make him so late. He told them about finding the extra forty yen, and he told them about returning to the man's shop. He told them everything—but he didn't tell them about the strange, secret voice in his head, and he did not tell them about giving the candy to the man's sick grandson. Why? Taro just felt like keeping those things to himself.

"May I have a candy now?" he asked.

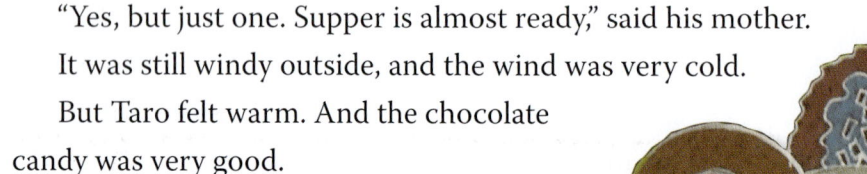

"Yes, but just one. Supper is almost ready," said his mother.

It was still windy outside, and the wind was very cold.

But Taro felt warm. And the chocolate candy was very good.

ABOUT THE AUTHOR

Masako Matsuno grew up in Japan. When she was 23, she came to America to study American children's literature. She has written books in both English and Japanese, translated Japanese books for American children, and translated English books for Japanese children. Mrs. Matsuno wants children all over the world to understand her people. She says, "The Japanese children like playing, eating, singing, and many other things just as foreign children do." Mrs. Matsuno enjoys gardening, reading, music, and taking walks.

Studying the Selection

FIRST IMPRESSIONS
Is it always easy to know what choice to make?

QUICK REVIEW
1. Why did Taro have to go to the tofu shop?
2. What mistake did the shopkeeper make?
3. What were two good reasons not to return the coin right away?
4. What was one bad reason not to return the coin?

FOCUS
5. Which of the "little voices'" arguments made Taro decide to run back and return the money immediately? Why?
6. Did Taro have to return the money, even though the tofu seller did not realize he had given him too much change? What do you think?

CREATING AND WRITING
7. In the story, the shopkeeper was very impressed by Taro's honesty. Imagine that the shopkeeper wrote Taro a thank you note for returning the money, and enclosed a small gift with the note. On a sheet of paper, write the kind of thank you note that the shopkeeper might have written. At the bottom of the paper, draw a picture of the gift that you think he might have given Taro.
8. Do you know what a diorama is? It is a model of a scene from a story or a real life event. Dioramas are often made by placing miniature dolls, furniture, and other scenery in a shoe box. The story of *Taro and the Tofu* takes place in several different locations. At first, Taro is at home. Then he runs through the streets to the tofu shop. Next, he is inside the tofu shop. Later he goes to the candy store, then back to the tofu shop, and then finally, back home. Bring a shoe box to school and choose one of the scenes in the story for your diorama. Your teacher will provide you with arts and crafts materials to use for your diorama. Design and make the scene, including figures of Taro and another character.

unit 1 wrap-up

all about the story!

ACTIVITY ONE

The stories in Unit One take you to many places. *The Jar of Tassai* takes place on a mesa near the Painted Desert in Arizona; *The Story of the White Sombrero* takes you to Mexico; *A Cane in Her Hand* takes you to an unnamed city in America; *Boom Town* takes you to the California of the 1850s; *Taro and the Tofu* takes you to Japan. Your teacher will provide you with some pictures of each location and materials for making a poster. Choose one of the stories in Unit One and design a travel poster for the story's location. Add a slogan like "Come Join Us in Japan!" or "A Golden Opportunity Awaits You in California!" If you wish, your poster can be three-dimensional. For example, you could use little orange balls to paste onto a drawing of an orange tree in Mexico.

The Jar of Tassai

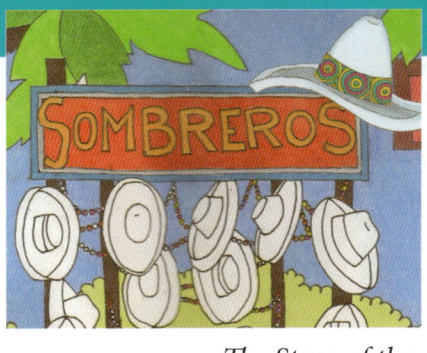

The Story of the White Sombrero

A Cane in Her Hand

Boom Town

Taro and the Tofu

ACTIVITY TWO
What Did You See?

1. Your teacher will ask you to sit in a circle.
2. The teacher will choose three to five stories from Unit One to use for this game.
3. The game starts when the first person says, "I read *The Story of the White Sombrero*, and this is what I saw: I saw *wasps*." The student must name one detail from the story. The next student repeats, "I read *The Story of the White Sombrero* and this is what I saw …" and adds a new thing.
4. Whenever a student cannot think of something else to add, the student must drop out of the circle.
5. The next student starts a new story.
6. The last person to remain in the circle is the winner.

wrap-up continued

ACTIVITY THREE

Who Am I?

1. Your teacher will choose five students to represent the main character in each of the five stories in Unit One: Tassai, Andres, Valerie, Amanda, and Taro.

2. The five students will be seated in a row in front of the classroom. They will keep which character each is representing a secret.

3. Your teacher will now divide the rest of the class into groups. The groups will take turns asking questions to the students sitting in the front to help uncover their "identities." Each group gets to ask two questions per round.

4. At the end of five rounds, a student from each group will stand up and "identify" each of the five students in the front. Then, the "characters" will stand up and identify themselves. The group with the most correct answers wins.

Here's an example: Mike is playing Andres and Leah is playing Tassai. One student asks: "Mike, do you know how to ride a burro?" Mike answers, "Yes." It looks like Mike might be Andres. A second student asks, "Leah, can you make pottery?" Leah says, "No." Leah is probably not Tassai.

ACTIVITY FOUR
Advice Column

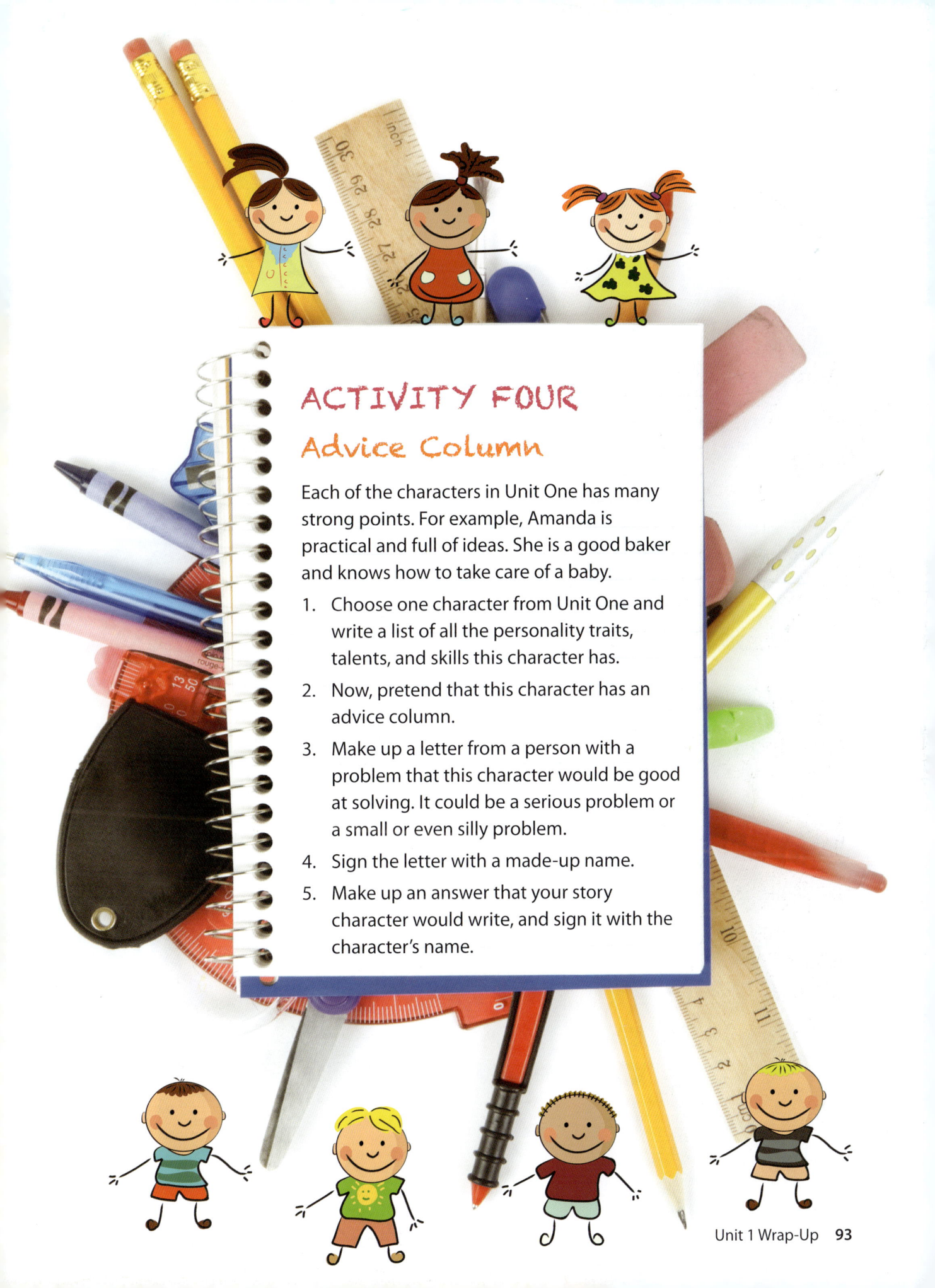

Each of the characters in Unit One has many strong points. For example, Amanda is practical and full of ideas. She is a good baker and knows how to take care of a baby.

1. Choose one character from Unit One and write a list of all the personality traits, talents, and skills this character has.
2. Now, pretend that this character has an advice column.
3. Make up a letter from a person with a problem that this character would be good at solving. It could be a serious problem or a small or even silly problem.
4. Sign the letter with a made-up name.
5. Make up an answer that your story character would write, and sign it with the character's name.

unit 2

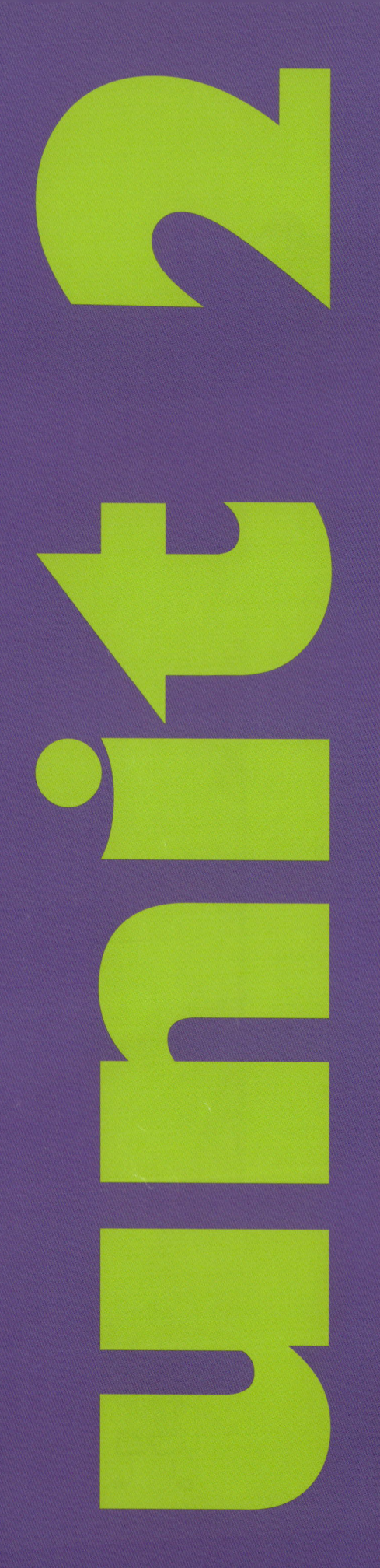

all about the plot!

THE UNKNOWN

NEW BEGINNINGS

MISUNDERSTANDINGS

ACTION

ADVENTURE

SILLINESS

Lesson in Literature...
The Cousin

WHAT IS INTERNAL CONFLICT?

- A **conflict** is a struggle. Most stories have a conflict that must be resolved, or settled.
- A conflict can be between two people or between a person and something else, like a fire, or the weather, or a wild animal.
- A conflict can also take place inside a person's own mind. That type of conflict is called an **internal**, or inner, **conflict**.
- Internal conflicts may occur when a character must choose between right and wrong.

THINK ABOUT IT!

1. What problem does Jeremy have at the beginning of the story?
2. Towards the end of the story, Jeremy has an internal conflict. He has to choose between two ways he can treat his cousin. What are the two ways?
3. Which choice does Jeremy make? Is he happy with his choice?

My name is Jeremy. I live with my parents on our farm in northern Vermont. I am ten years old. I have no brothers or sisters. Even when you are ten, you can feel lonely.

A while ago, I asked my mom why I'm an only child. That is what people call it when you have no brothers or sisters: an only child. She sighed, "Jeremy, it is difficult to explain. But *you* make us very happy. It is a blessing just having *you*."

As I said, I have been lonely. But I am used to the way things are.

We have a dog named Lucy. We also have several horses that are good horses for riding. Mine is Patience. When I began riding, I was really clumsy. That was when Patience earned her name. My dad's horse is Jackson, my mom's is Gloria. Their baby is Little Boy. He's too young to ride.

Two weeks ago, my parents said they had something to tell me. It sounded like it was going to be a good thing. Then they said my cousin Will was coming to live with us. "Forever?" I asked. "Where will he sleep?"

Dad said, "Well, we figured you two would share your room. Will's your age. And you had a good time when he visited us from Quebec last January."

"But he came with his own mom and dad then. A visitor is different from a permanent extra person. He is not part of our family."

Mom sort of groaned. "Look, Jeremy. Will's mom is sick. His dad works far away from Quebec in Ontario. Will *is* a family member. His mom is my sister. She needs our help."

I felt miserable. I didn't want to share my mom and dad. I didn't want to share my room or even my horse. I didn't want to share Lucy either. I couldn't remember why I had liked Will.

When my mom and dad went to pick him up at the train station, I said I wasn't going. They both stared at me, like they were shocked. "Look, I have a lot of homework! Isn't it better if I finish it before he gets here?"

Will is here now. He doesn't look happy. I never thought that he might not like this either. But I can't worry about him. I have to worry about me.

My mom shows him the extra dresser in my room. He unpacks. I sit there not speaking.

Then he says, "I brought you a geode. It looks like a rock on the outside, but when you open it, it's purple crystals that sparkle." I think, why do I need an old rock? Will hands it to me, like we're some kind of buddies.

I want to hand it back to him and leave the room, but I can't do that. Mom and Dad would think it was a really ugly thing to do. So, I open it. It is really cool!

It's hard for me to say it, but I ask him which bunk bed he wants, the top or the bottom. He says, "Don't you always sleep on top?"

"Yeah, but you choose. It's probably hard leaving home and all."

"Well, I'll take the bottom. You know, fear of heights." We both laugh at that.

Mom yells from the kitchen. "Hey, I've got apples here. Why don't you two go and give one to each of the horses? And the pony, too—little pieces."

We step outside into the chill October air clutching our apples. "Race you to the barn!" I shout to Will. "Loser is a rotten egg!"

Maybe this isn't going to be so bad after all.

Good-Bye, 382 Shin Dang Dong

Blueprint for Reading

INTO . . . *Good-Bye, 382 Shin Dang Dong*

Do you like change or do you like things to stay the same? Some people are adventurers and they love setting out for places they've never seen. Other people love what is familiar and would like it if they never had to leave home for very long. Jangmi is a Korean girl who moved to America when she was eight years old. She remembers how sad and frightened she was of leaving her home, her friends, and her country. Yet, she'd had no choice. As the taxi carried the family to the airport, Jangmi cried. What could you say that would comfort or encourage Jangmi?

EYES ON *Internal Conflict*

Every plot includes at least some conflict. **Conflict** is disagreement of any sort. If you want to go outside and play, but your teacher makes you stay inside, that is a conflict. If you want to go outside and it is raining—that is also a conflict. If you want to go outside and play, but your friend must stay inside and will feel lonely, one part of you may say "don't go." That's a conflict, too. This kind of conflict is all in your mind, and you have to decide what to do. It is called **internal conflict**.

Jangmi faces two conflicts. The first one is easy to spot. She wants to stay in her home in Korea, but she must move with her family to America. The second conflict is inside herself. Should she let herself feel sad for a long time, or should she let go of her sadness and try to find happiness in her new country?

Good-Bye, 382 Shin Dang Dong

Frances Park and Ginger Park

My heart beats in two places: Here, where I live, and also in a place where I once lived. You see, I was born in Korea. One day my parents told me we were moving to America. I was eight years old, old enough to keep many lovely memories of my birthplace alive in my heart forever. But one very sad memory stays with me too. The day I cried, "Good-bye, 382 Shin Dang Dong!"

On that summer day I woke up to the sound of light rain tapping on my window. The monsoon season[1] was coming. I didn't even need to open my eyes to know that. It was that time of year. It was also time to move.

In a few hours, I would be on an airplane.

When I opened my eyes, my heart sank. My bedroom was so bare! No hand-painted scrolls or colorful fans on my walls. No silk cushions or straw mats on my floor. All my possessions were packed away in a big brown box marked "Lovely Things."

I frowned and listened to the raindrops. One, two, three … Soon the thick of the monsoon would arrive, and a thousand raindrops would hit our clay-tiled roof all at once. But I wouldn't be here to listen to them. I would be halfway around the world in a strange, foreign place called 112 Foster Terrace, Brighton, Massachusetts, U.S.A.

---

1. A *monsoon* is a strong wind that blows in from the ocean, bringing heavy rain. The *monsoon season* is the part of the year when it is extremely windy and rainy in certain countries.

My parents were very excited.

"Jangmi,[2] you will like America," Dad tried to assure me.

"Are the seasons the same?" I wondered.

"Oh, yes."

"With monsoon rains?"

"No, Jangmi, no monsoon rains."

"No friends either," I moaned.

"You will make many new friends in America," Mom promised me, "in your new home."

But I loved my home right here! I didn't want to go to America and make new friends. I didn't want to leave my best friend, Kisuni.[3]

---

2. *Jangmi* (JAHNG MEE)
3. *Kisuni* (KEE soo NEE)

After breakfast, Kisuni and I ran out into the rain and to the open market. Monsoon season was also the season for sweet, yellow melons called *chummy*. Kisuni and I would often peel and eat chummy under the willow tree that stood outside my bedroom window. But today, the chummy were for guests who were coming over for a farewell lunch.

At the market we peered into endless baskets and took our time choosing the ripest, plumpest chummy we could find.

"Do they have chummy in America?" Kisuni wondered.

"No," I replied. "But my mom says they have melons called *honeydew*."

"Honeydew," Kisuni giggled. "What a funny name!"

Soon after we returned, family and friends began to arrive, carrying pots and plates of food. One by one they took off their shoes, then entered the house. Grandmother was dressed in her most special occasion *hanbok*.[4] She set up the long *bap sang*[5] and before I could even blink, on it were a big pot of dumpling soup and the prettiest pastel rice cakes I had ever seen. Kisuni and I peeled and sliced our chummy and carefully arranged the pieces on a plate.

Then everybody ate and sang traditional Korean songs and celebrated in a sad way. Love and laughter and tears rippled through our house. How I wanted to pack these moments into a big brown box and bring them with me to America.

Kisuni and I sneaked outside and sat beneath the willow tree. We watched the rain with glum faces.

---

4. A *hanbok* (HAHN BOK) robe is an outer robe worn in traditional Korean dress.
5. A *bap sang* (BOP SANG) is a table on which a variety of dishes are served, similar to a buffet.

"Kisuni, I wish we never had to move from this spot," I said.

"Me, too," she sighed. "Jangmi, how far away is America?"

"My mom says that it's halfway around the world. And my dad told me that when the moon is shining here, the sun is shining there. That's how far apart we'll be," I moaned.

"That's really far," Kisuni moaned back.

We watched the rain and grew more glum than ever. Then Kisuni perked up.

"So when you're awake, I'll be asleep. And when I'm awake, you'll be asleep," she declared. "At least we'll always know what the other one is doing."

That moment our faces brightened. But a moment later we had to say good-bye.

Kisuni held back her tears. "Promise you'll write to me, Jangmi."

"I promise, Kisuni."

It was time to go to the airport.

"Kimpo Airport," Dad instructed the taxi driver.

The taxi slowly pulled away. I looked at our beautiful home one last time. Like rain on the window, tears streaked down my face.

"Good-bye, 382 Shin Dang Dong!" I cried.

On the long ride to the airport, Dad asked me, "Do you want to know what your new home looks like?"

"Okay," I shrugged.

"Let's see," Dad began, "it's a row house."

"A house that's attached to other houses," Mom explained.

"And inside the house are wooden floors," Dad added.

"No *ondal* floors?" I asked him. "How will we keep warm in the winter without ondal floors?"

"There are radiators in every room!" Mom said with an enthusiastic clap. "And a fireplace in the living room! Imagine!"

No, I could not imagine that. In our home we had a fire in the cellar called the *ondal*. It stayed lit all the time. The heat from the ondal traveled through underground pipes and kept our wax-covered floors warm and cozy. A fireplace in the living room sounded peculiar to me.

"And the rooms are separated by wooden doors," Mom added.

"No rice-paper doors?" I wondered.

My parents shook their heads. "No, Jangmi."

My eyes closed with disappointment. I had a hard time picturing this house. Would it ever feel like home?

Word Bank
radiator (RAY dee AY ter) *n.*: a room heater made of pipes through which steam or hot water passes
enthusiastic (en THOOZ ee AS tik) *adj.*: excited and eager

On the airplane, I sat by the window. We flew over rice fields and clay-tiled roofs. Already I felt homesick.

The next thing I knew, we were flying over the ocean. At first I could see fishing boats rocking in the waters. As we climbed higher and higher into the clouds, the boats grew smaller and smaller. Suddenly, the world looked very big to me.

"Good-bye, 382 Shin Dang Dong," I cried again.

Dad sat back in his seat and began to read an American newspaper. The words were all foreign.

"Dad," I asked, "how will I ever learn to understand English?"

"It's not so hard," he said. "Would you like to learn an English word?"

"Okay," I sighed.

After a pause, Dad came up with—

"Rose."

"Rose?" I repeated. "What does that mean?"

"That's the English translation of your Korean name," Mom said.

"Rose means Jangmi?" I asked.

"Yes," my parents nodded.

"Rose," I said over and over.

"Would you like to adopt Rose as your American name?" Mom asked me.

"No, I like *my* name," I insisted.

On a foggy morning four days later, we arrived in Massachusetts. After we gathered our luggage, we climbed into an airport taxi.

Even through the fog, I could see that things were very different in America. There were big, wide roads called *highways*. The rooftops were shingled instead of clay-tiled. People shopped in glass-enclosed stores instead of open markets. No rice fields, no monsoon rains. So many foreign faces.

Slowly, the taxi pulled up to a row house on a quiet street. Red brick steps led up to a wooden door.

"Here we are, Jangmi," Dad said, "112 Foster Terrace, Brighton, Massachusetts, U.S.A."

Good-Bye, 382 Shin Dang Dong

The house was just as my parents had described. I took off my shoes and walked on wooden floors. They felt very cold. I opened wooden doors. They felt very heavy. Outside, the fog had lifted. But inside, everything felt dark and strange.

"Look," Dad pointed out the window, "there's a tree just like the one at home."

"No, it's not, Dad. It's not a willow tree," I said.

"No," he agreed. "It's a maple tree. But isn't it beautiful?"

382 Shin Dang Dong, 382 Shin Dang Dong. I wanted to go home to 382 Shin Dang Dong right now. Only a knock at the door saved me from tears.

112   Unit 2

Mom announced, "The movers are here!"

The house quickly filled up with furniture and big brown boxes. The box marked "Lovely Things" was the last to arrive.

I unpacked all my possessions. I hung my hand-painted scrolls and colorful fans on the walls. I placed my silk cushions and straw mats on the floor.

Then came another knock. To our surprise a parade of neighbors waltzed in[6] carrying plates of curious food. There were pink-and-white iced cakes and warm pans containing something called *casseroles*.

A girl my age wandered up to me with a small glass bowl. Inside the bowl were colorful balls. They smelled fruity.

She pointed to a red ball and said, "Watermelon!" She pointed to an orange ball and said, "Cantaloupe!" Lastly she pointed to a green ball and said, "Honeydew!"

I took a green ball and tasted it. Mmm … it was as sweet and delicious as chummy.

The girl asked me a question. But I couldn't understand her.

"She wants to know what kind of fruit you eat in Korea," Dad stepped in.

"Chummy," I replied.

"Chummy," the girl repeated, then giggled—just like Kisuni!

She asked me another question.

"She wants to know your name," Dad said.

---

6. *Waltzed in* is an expression that means they came in happily and confidently.

Maybe someday I would adopt Rose as my American name. But not today.

"Jangmi," I replied.

"Jangmi," the girl smiled. "My name is Mary."

"Mary," I smiled back.

I had made a new friend.

Later, when all the guests had gone, I went outside and sat under the maple tree. Dad was right, it *was* beautiful. Maybe someday Mary and I would sit beneath this tree and watch the rain fall. And maybe I would come to love it as much as our willow tree back home in Korea. But not today.

I began to write.

Dear Kisuni …

My best friend was so far away from me. So very, very far. But at least I knew where Kisuni was and what she was doing. She was halfway around the world, sleeping to the sound of a thousand raindrops hitting her clay-tiled roof all at once.

About the Authors

Frances and Ginger Park are sisters who grew up in Virginia. They were the only Korean-American family they knew in their town. Writing books about children emigrating from Korea has helped Frances and Ginger connect to the country their parents left. Frances and Ginger Park both love tennis and chocolate. In addition to writing books together, the sisters own a chocolate store in Washington, D.C. They say that the store is a very fun place to be when they are not writing.

New Kid at School

Betsy Franco

Where did you come from?
Far away.
Miss your friends?
Every day.
Where do you live?
Maple Street.
What's your name?
Call me Pete.

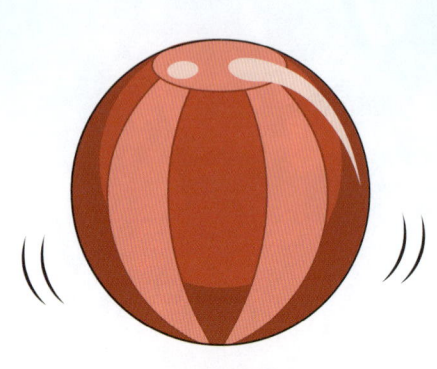

How old are you?
Just turned eight.
You like hoops?
Yeah, great.
Got any friends?
Nope, not yet.
Wanna play?
You bet!

Studying the Selection

FIRST IMPRESSIONS
Jangmi has to leave her house, her friends, and her country. Will anywhere else ever feel like home?

QUICK REVIEW
1. What is Shin Dang Dong?
2. What season was it when Jangmi left Korea?
3. What does the name Jangmi mean?
4. What happened in Massachusetts to make Jangmi feel much less lonely?

FOCUS
5. Explain how the weather conditions may have added to Jangmi's emotions as she left Korea.
6. At the end of the story, Jangmi's feelings have changed. Compare how she felt when she was in the taxi on the way to the airport to the way she felt after Mary introduced herself.

CREATING AND WRITING
7. The days following Jangmi's arrival in Massachusetts were filled with activity. She had to unpack, register at her new school, and meet many new people, both children and adults. Imagine that you are Jangmi and that you are writing a letter to your friend Kisuni in Korea. In your letter, describe everything that has happened in the last few days, including how you've been feeling and how much you've missed her.
8. Jangmi packed a box of "Lovely Things" to take with her to America. Everyone has some treasured items. Choose three or four things that are very special to you and put them in a box. Prepare to show the objects to your class and explain why they are meaningful to you.

Lesson in Literature...
THE UNDERGROUND ROAD

WHAT IS EXTERNAL CONFLICT?
- **External** means outside.
- When the conflict in a story is between a character and something outside the character, it is called an **external conflict**.
- What is *outside* the character? It could be anything with which a character struggles. A storm, an enemy, or a rattlesnake are some examples.
- An external conflict is not necessarily a struggle between right and wrong. It is simply a struggle. For example, a story's external conflict could be about a man trying to keep his ship from sinking during a storm.

THINK ABOUT IT!
1. What is Tice Davids struggling against?
2. Who offers to help Tice with his struggle?
3. How is the struggle—the external conflict—resolved?

The year was 1831. A young man was on his knees, digging in the dirt. He was planting some seeds in the dry soil. It was midday. He was hot and thirsty.

His name was Tice Davids. He worked and lived on a plantation in Kentucky near the Ohio River. Tice had been born a slave.

He didn't know how old he was. He didn't even know the month or day he was born. He couldn't remember his momma. She had been sold to a slaveholder in Alabama when he was a baby, so he couldn't ask her how old he was.

Tice had no family. His brother and sister had been sold. So had Robert, his best friend when he was seven. He missed his grandma. About a year before, she had been given as a present to an old white woman. The old white woman needed a companion.

The work in the fields was very hard. He toiled and sweated in the sun from early morning until the sun went down. His clothes were like rags. He slept on the floor of a tiny hut. Even though he was young, he felt so tired.

Always, he tried to do what he was told. He didn't want to be hurt.

What would it be like not to be owned? Sometimes he could feel how odd it was— that a person could be bought or sold. Other times it just seemed this was the way life was.

Some days he felt he just couldn't stand to be a slave. He had thoughts that were dangerous thoughts. He could never say what he was thinking to anyone.

But he kept on having the same thoughts. He listened to the other slaves when they whispered. How did they know which way to go? He didn't have a map to tell him. He wasn't sure he knew what a map was. He had never seen one. Besides, he couldn't read. Slaves weren't allowed to learn to read.

Tice didn't own anything except a smooth pebble he had found. Was there anything he would need to bring with him? He didn't have anything to bring. What would he eat? How far could he go? Would someone help him?

Then Joseph, the wrinkled old man with white hair, spoke softly to Tice one night. "Boy," he sighed, "you got that look on you. What you do, you cross the river. Then run up that hill. You be in Ripley. Ripley hates slavery. The house on the hilltop belongs to the Reverend and Mrs. Rankin. A lantern shines from the window. That be your first stop." Then he walked away. Joseph didn't speak to him again.

Tice waited for a night when there was no moon. Then he slipped away quietly. He ran like crazy through the chill night air. He tripped on a rock and nearly fell, and slid into the icy waters of the Ohio. He could hear the men and the dogs after him. He could hear his heart beating madly as he swam for his life. He reached the Ohio shore.

His white master wasn't far behind. He rowed furiously across the river that separated the free state of Ohio from the slave state of Kentucky. He searched the banks of the Ohio for a long time. Tice had vanished.

His owner returned empty-handed to Kentucky. He was very angry. It is said that he muttered, "It's like he disappeared. That boy must have gone on some underground road."

Sybil Rides By Night   119

Blueprint for Reading

INTO . . . *Sybil Rides By Night*

Sybil was a teenager whose father was a colonel in the American Army during the Revolutionary War. One night, when most teenagers were sleeping soundly in their beds, Sybil mounted her horse, Star, and took off into the night to warn the men in the neighboring towns that the British were coming. It was dark, it was rainy, it was cold, and it was scary. Would you want to be in her shoes? As you ride with Sybil, ask yourself: Would I, *could* I, do what she did?

EYES ON *External Conflict*

In *Good-Bye, 382 Shin Dang Dong* we learned about *internal conflict*, which is a struggle that takes place inside a person's mind. *Sybil Rides By Night* has a conflict, too, but this time it is between the main character and something *outside* of her. There is Sybil, on one side, and the dangers of the nighttime ride, on the other side. The struggle between the two sides is called **external conflict**. As you read, see if you can guess which side—Sybil or the dangers she faces—will come out the winner.

Sybil Rides By Night

From *Sybil Rides for Independence*

Drollene P. Brown

A young girl named Sybil turned sixteen as the American colonies struggled for independence. Although girls her age were expected to bake, sew, and keep house, Sybil preferred to ride her horse, Star, and to hear about the colonial soldiers and their battles. Sybil's father, Henry Ludington, was a commander in the colonial army. On the night of April 26, 1777, Colonel Ludington got a message: The British had marched to a nearby town, Danbury, and set it afire. If no one stopped them, they would continue marching from town to town, destroying everything in their path. American soldiers had to be rounded up from their farms to fight the British. Who would take that dangerous job? Who knew where each of the farmers lived and was courageous enough to ride through the dark, cold, rainy night? Who would dare to go where British soldiers and outlaws roamed?

Colonel Ludington knew of one such person: his daughter, Sybil. Excited and frightened, Sybil agreed to ride by night.

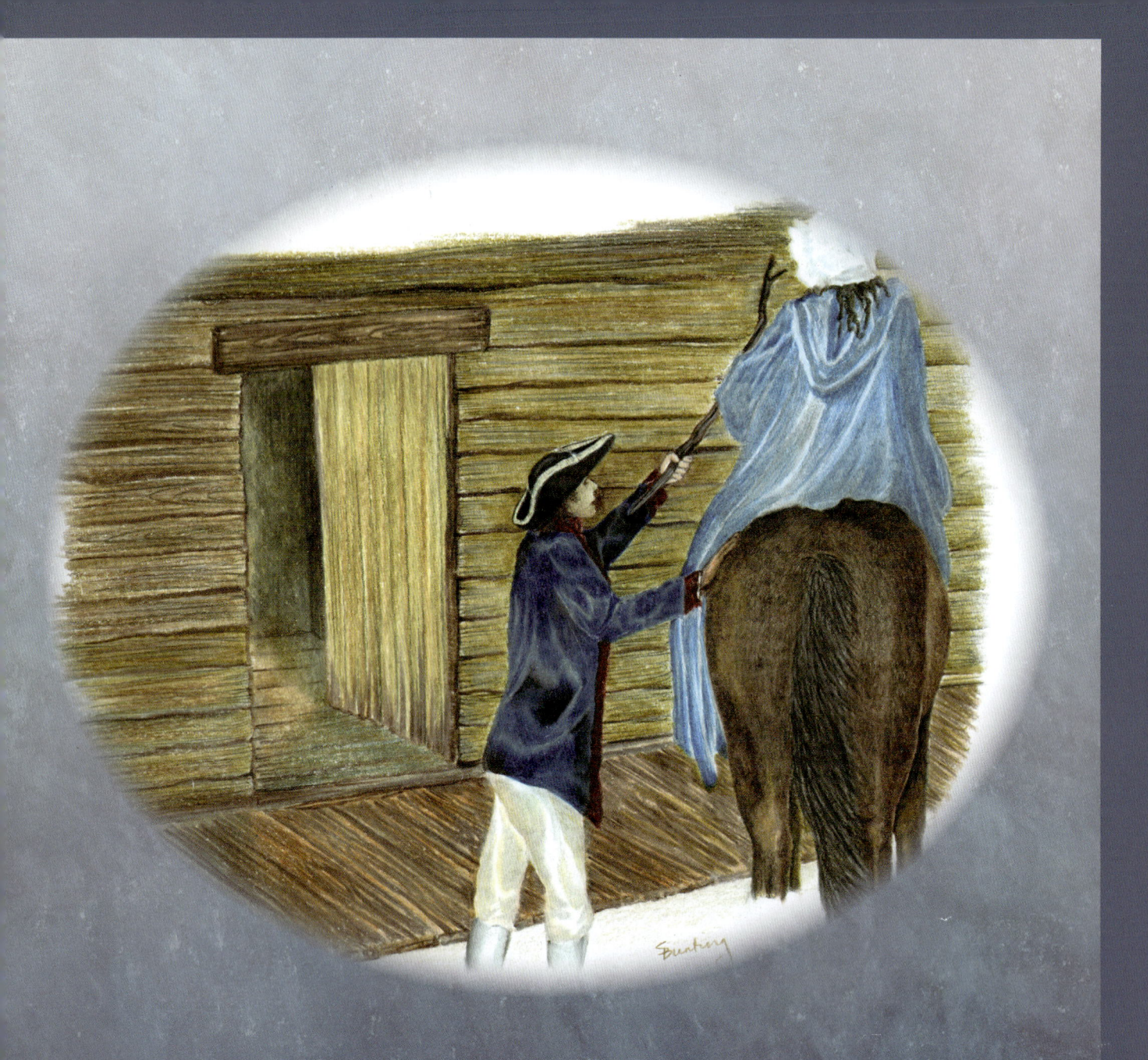

Sybil swung up on Star. She patted his neck and leaned toward his ear. "This ride is for freedom," she whispered.

The colonel[1] looked up at his daughter. He handed her a big stick. "Listen for others on the path," he warned. "Pull off and hide if you hear hoofbeats or footsteps or voices.

"You know where to go. Tell our men that Danbury's burning. Tell them to gather at Ludingtons'." Sybil listened to her orders. She saluted her father, her colonel. He stepped back and returned the salute.

---

1. A *colonel* is an officer in the U.S. Army, Air Force, or Marine Corps, ranking above lieutenant colonel.

Sybil thought of what might happen. There were more than thirty miles to cover in the dark and rain. She could be lost or hurt or caught by Redcoats![2] But she did not let these black thoughts scare her. *I will do it for the colonies,*[3] she vowed.

She turned Star south on a line with the river. There would be several lone farmhouses to alert before they reached Shaw's Pond.

It was almost eight o'clock when she reached the first farmhouse. Doors flew open at the sound of Star's hoofbeats.

Sybil shouted her message. She did not stop, but hurried on to the farmhouses that were along Horse Pound Road. It was about ten o'clock when Sybil reached Shaw's Pond.

The houses beside the water were dark for the night. Sybil hadn't thought of this. She had been so excited she had forgotten people would be sleeping.

---

2. Before and during the War for Independence, the British soldiers were called *Redcoats*, for the simple reason that their uniform jackets were red.
3. Before the United States gained their independence from Great Britain, they were called *the colonies*. The thirteen colonies were the first thirteen states.

Sybil Rides By Night

Sybil stopped for only a moment. She coaxed Star up to the door and pounded with her stick.

A window opened. A head poked out. "Look to the east!" Sybil shouted. "Danbury's burning! Gather at Ludingtons'!"

She did not beat on every door. She did not shout at every house. Neighbors called to each other; and in the little hamlets along her way, one of the first ones awakened rushed out to ring the town bell.

When the alarm began to sound, Sybil would stop her shouting and ride on into the darkness.

Her throat hurt from calling out her message. Her heart beat wildly, and her tired eyes burned. Her skirt seemed to be filled with heavy weights, for

Word Bank

coaxed (KOKST) *v.*: gently tried to get someone to do something

it was wet and caked with mud. She pulled her mother's cloak closer against the cold and rain that would not stop.

Sybil would not stop, either. All the soldiers in the regiment must be told. She urged Star on.

Outside the village at Mahopac[4] Pond, Star slipped in the mud. He got up right away, but Sybil's eyes stung with tears. She would have to be more careful!

If Star were hurt, she would blame herself. She must walk Star over loose rocks and pick through the underbrush where there was no path.

Again and again, Sybil woke up sleeping soldiers. Nearing Red Mills, Star stumbled and almost fell. He was breathing heavily. "You are fine, Star," Sybil whispered.

---

4. *Mahopac* (mah HO puk)

Sybil looked at the sky. The moon was half-risen. That meant it was well past midnight. She guessed they were halfway through, but the long ride to Stormville still lay ahead.

More slowly now, they started on their way. Then—hoofbeats on the path! Quickly Sybil reined Star to a halt. She jumped down and pulled him toward the trees.

She held her breath and strained her eyes. Men passed so close she could have touched them. They looked like British soldiers, but sometimes

> **WORD BANK**
>
> **strained** *v.*: tried to make them work even better than they usually did

skinners[5] dressed like soldiers of one army or the other to fool the people they robbed.

Soon the hoofbeats died away. Sybil's hands and knees trembled as she guided Star back to the path.

"We'll make it," she softly promised him. Star pricked up his ears and started off again. He was weary, but he trusted Sybil.

When they reached Stormville, the alarm had already begun to sound. Someone from another village had come with the news. Sybil was glad, for she could only whisper. She had shouted away her voice.

---

5. During the Revolutionary War, groups of bandits roamed the countryside and robbed both the British and the Americans. They were called *skinners*.

Covered with mud, horse and rider turned home. When Sybil rode into her yard, more than four hundred men were ready to march. She looked at the eastern sky. It was red.

"Is Danbury still burning?" she asked and tumbled into Father's arms.

"No, my brave soldier. It is the sunrise. You have ridden all night."

"I do not feel like a brave soldier," Sybil whispered. "I feel like a very tired girl. Star needs care," she murmured sleepily as she was carried to her bed.

Early that morning, while that very tired girl slept, her father's men joined soldiers from Connecticut. They met the British at Ridgefield, about ten miles from Danbury.

The soldiers from New York and Connecticut battled with the Redcoats. Most of the British escaped to their ships in Long Island Sound, but they did no further damage.

People spread the word of Sybil's ride. Soon General Washington came to her house to thank her for her courage. Statesman Alexander Hamilton wrote to her, praising her deed.

America was soon a growing, changing nation, and Sybil's life changed, too. At twenty-three she married Edmond Ogden. They had six children, and she kept house. She baked, she mended, and she washed the dishes.

Sybil Rides By Night

But sometimes she would stop in the middle of a chore. Remembering that cold, wet night in 1777, she would shiver again. Then warm feelings of pride would fill her as she thought, "Once I was brave for my country."

Sybil lived to be seventy-eight years old. Her children and her children's children loved to hear the story of a young girl's ride for independence.

> **WORD BANK**
> **independence** (IN dih PEN dunce) *n.*: freedom; the right to think and act for oneself

ABOUT THE AUTHOR

Drollene P. Brown has been writing ever since she was a child. When she was in school, she would write papers for fun and give them to her teachers to grade. When she got older, she went through many careers, including college professor, banker, editor, writer, book store manager, and business consultant. Mrs. Brown wants to make a difference to people and she loves visiting schools to talk about writing and about her books.

Studying the Selection

FIRST IMPRESSIONS
If there was no adult available to do a dangerous job, would you have the confidence and the courage to do it?

QUICK REVIEW

1. What message was Sybil supposed to deliver to the soldiers?
2. What happened at Shaw Pond that Sybil had not expected?
3. Some riders passed Sybil and Star. Who could they have been?
4. What happened in the battle at Ridgefield?

FOCUS

5. Sybil had powerful feelings that gave her the courage to ride through the night. List three strong beliefs or feelings Sybil had that gave her the strength to keep going.
6. In a conflict, one or more things are working against the main character. List at least three things with which Sybil had to struggle during her ride.

CREATING AND WRITING

7. Pretend that you are a neighbor of the Ludingtons and the *Colonial Gazette* has asked you to write a news item about Sybil's ride. They would like an article that includes details like what snacks Mrs. Ludington sent with Sybil, how Sybil's dog howled for an hour after she left, and so on. Write a long paragraph that includes a lot of interesting (made-up) details. Make sure you have an exciting headline, too.
8. People want to honor the heroes who helped our country win its independence. One way to do that is by putting their names and faces on coins or bills. Another way to remember them is by putting their names, faces, or some symbol of their deeds on a stamp. Using the materials provided by your teacher, design a 99 cent coin or a 50 cent stamp to honor Sybil Ludington.

Lesson in Literature...
MOM I LOVE YOU

WHAT IS SEQUENCE?

- **Sequence** means order. For example, to list the days of the week in their proper sequence, you would say, "Sunday, Monday, Tuesday," and so on.
- In most stories, the events are described in sequence, the order in which they happened.
- At times, a story will have a flashback, or jump ahead into the future. These events are out of sequence.
- Sequence is especially important in lists, recipes, and instructions.

THINK ABOUT IT!

1. How many days before Mother's Day did Charlie write on the wall?
2. On which day did Mom see the writing on the wall?
3. Put the following events in their proper sequence:
   a. Mother's Day
   b. Charlie writes a note to his mother and makes her a snack.
   c. Charlie sees his mother packing his clothes.
   d. Eleanor sees the writing on the wall.
   e. There is screaming and crying.

Charlie and Eleanor were brother and sister. They were also good friends. Usually, Charlie and Eleanor agreed about things. But when Mother's Day was just around the corner, Charlie had a great idea that he did not share with Eleanor. He did not know where or how he got this idea. It just came over him like a thunderbolt.

Mother's Day was on Sunday. The Wednesday before Mother's Day, he wrote in large letters on his wall,

MOM I LOVE YOU!

This wall had recently been wallpapered. Yet Charlie proceeded, without giving this any thought. He wanted his mother to know how much he loved her, so he wrote with a wide-tipped, black permanent marker. He didn't want the giant words to ever be washed away.

When Eleanor got home, he shouted down to her excitedly, "I'm up here! Wait till you see this!"

Eleanor came running up the stairs and burst into Charlie's room. "Oh my heavens!" she gasped. "Charlie!" She covered her face with her hands. "What are we going to do?!"

"Oh, Eleanor," he said. "Don't worry. I'll tell Mom you helped, too."

"Charlie," Eleanor whispered, "the walls were just done. I know you meant to do something nice, but this is really dreadful."

"Gosh, I thought Mom would be so pleased." Charlie looked a little confused. "Maybe you're wrong, El, maybe Mom will think it's very … special."

"Charlie, we need to see if we can get this off the wall. I can't even imagine what Mom and Dad will say."

When they tried to remove the writing, the wallpaper got wet and crumbly. "I don't know why I was so stupid," Charlie muttered. "I've done something terrible." Then Charlie got into bed. He didn't know what else to do.

Mom came home and made dinner. Dad got home at 6:00. Eleanor silently did her homework. Mom said, "Where's Charlie?"

Eleanor spoke with a sort of moan. "Mom, Charlie isn't feeling well. He went to bed."

"To bed?" Mom asked. "I better go up and check on him."

Eleanor waited and then she heard a shriek. There was screaming and crying. Dad looked over to her. "What's all that about, kiddo?" Eleanor felt she couldn't speak. Poor Charlie! Poor Mom!

Mom marched down the stairs. "What has happened to that boy?"

"Mom," Eleanor cried, "he just wanted to tell you he loves you."

"A fine way he has to show it!"

That night his mom didn't come and kiss him good night.

The next day at breakfast, Charlie couldn't look at his mom. He didn't know how to apologize for such a horrible mistake. After school, Eleanor tried to comfort him.

"Charlie, you will see. Everything will get worked out."

Charlie blurted, "I think they hate me now!"

Still, Charlie wrote his mother a note all in capital letters. This note was written on a piece of paper:

MOM, PLEASE FORGIVE ME. I'LL DO 100 CHORES FOR FREE.

I'LL GIVE UP MY ALLOWANCE AND TRY TO PAY YOU BACK.

Charlie made his mom a snack for when she got home: graham crackers with cream cheese and iced tea. He placed the note between the two small stacks of graham crackers. Then he went up to his room and did his homework.

At dinner Mom seemed a little cheerier. She thanked him for the snack and the note. But later on before bed, he saw his mom packing a suitcase with his fall clothes. Why would she be packing his clothes? Were they going to send him away to boarding school to live? He couldn't stand that—to be away from his family.

When his mom came into his room to kiss him good night, she sat down on the bed. She said, "We need to talk."

Charlie said, "You're going to tell me that you and Dad are going to send me away to boarding school!" Then he burst into tears.

His mom put her arms around him and held him in a strong hug. "Oh, you foolish boy. We would never send you away! How could we, when you are going to help us repaper the wall?"

Blueprint for Reading

INTO . . . *Nothing Much Happened Today*

Nothing much happens in this story except for … a policeman chasing a robber, a dog chasing a cat, a room filling with smoke, a million bubbles floating into the sky—and a few other little things. But don't worry, there's a good explanation for everything; read on and you'll see!

EYES ON *Sequence*

Have you ever seen a bowling ball hit one pin, which falls and hits another, which knocks over a few more, and results in a strike for the lucky bowler? If you have, then you have seen a *chain reaction*. Chain reactions can be funny or serious, helpful or destructive. Many gadgets and machines depend on chain reactions to make them work. But one thing that is shared by all chain reactions is that the events take place in a certain order, or **sequence**. The first event causes the second and the second causes the third, just the way the first bowling pin knocks over the second and the second one knocks over the third. As you read *Nothing Much Happened Today*, exercise your mind. Try to remember everything that happened in the story—*in order*!

Nothing Much Happened Today

Mrs. Maeberry held her groceries tightly. She scurried home to tell her children about seeing the police chase a robber. But when she turned down her sidewalk, her mouth flew open. Soap bubbles—hundreds, thousands, maybe millions of soap bubbles—were drifting from her front window. She ran inside. "What's happened?" she demanded. "What's happened here?"

Mary Blount Christian

Stephen shrugged. "Nothing much, really."

"But the bubbles!" she yelled. "Look at those bubbles!"

Stephen shrugged again.

Elizabeth mumbled, "I guess maybe we did use too many suds when we bathed Popsicle."

"The dog? You bathed the dog?" Mother screamed. "Why did you bathe the dog?"

"He got sugar stuck all over his fur," Alan, the youngest, said.

Mother set her groceries down. "I was gone five minutes. How could Popsicle get sugar in his fur?"

"He got sugar in his fur when he knocked over the sugar sack. That was when he was chasing the cat through the kitchen," Stephen added.

Mother gasped. "Cat? Cat? We don't *have* a cat."

"I guess you could say it was a visiting cat," Stephen explained. "It came through the window."

"The window?" Mother shrieked. "That cat broke the glass?"

Stephen shook his head. "Nope. The window was open. We had to let the smoke out."

138　Unit 2

Mother grabbed her forehead. "Smoke! What smoke?"

"The smoke from the oven when the cake batter spilled over," Elizabeth volunteered.

Mother waved her arms. "Why were you baking a cake?"

"For the school bake sale," Alan reminded her.

"But," Mother protested. "But I baked that before I went to the store."

"We know," Stephen said, "but that one got ruined."

"Ruined?" Mother repeated. "How could my beautiful cake get ruined? I was gone ten minutes, only ten minutes."

"The cake was knocked onto the floor, and it's a good thing it was, too," Elizabeth said.

"I don't understand this. I don't understand this at all," Mother said.

"It's not so bad," Stephen said. "We used too many soap suds on Popsicle because he was covered with sugar. He knocked the sugar over chasing the cat. The cat came through the window when we let out the smoke. The smoke is from the spilled cake batter in the oven. We were replacing the cake you baked because that one got knocked off by the police officer."

140 Unit 2

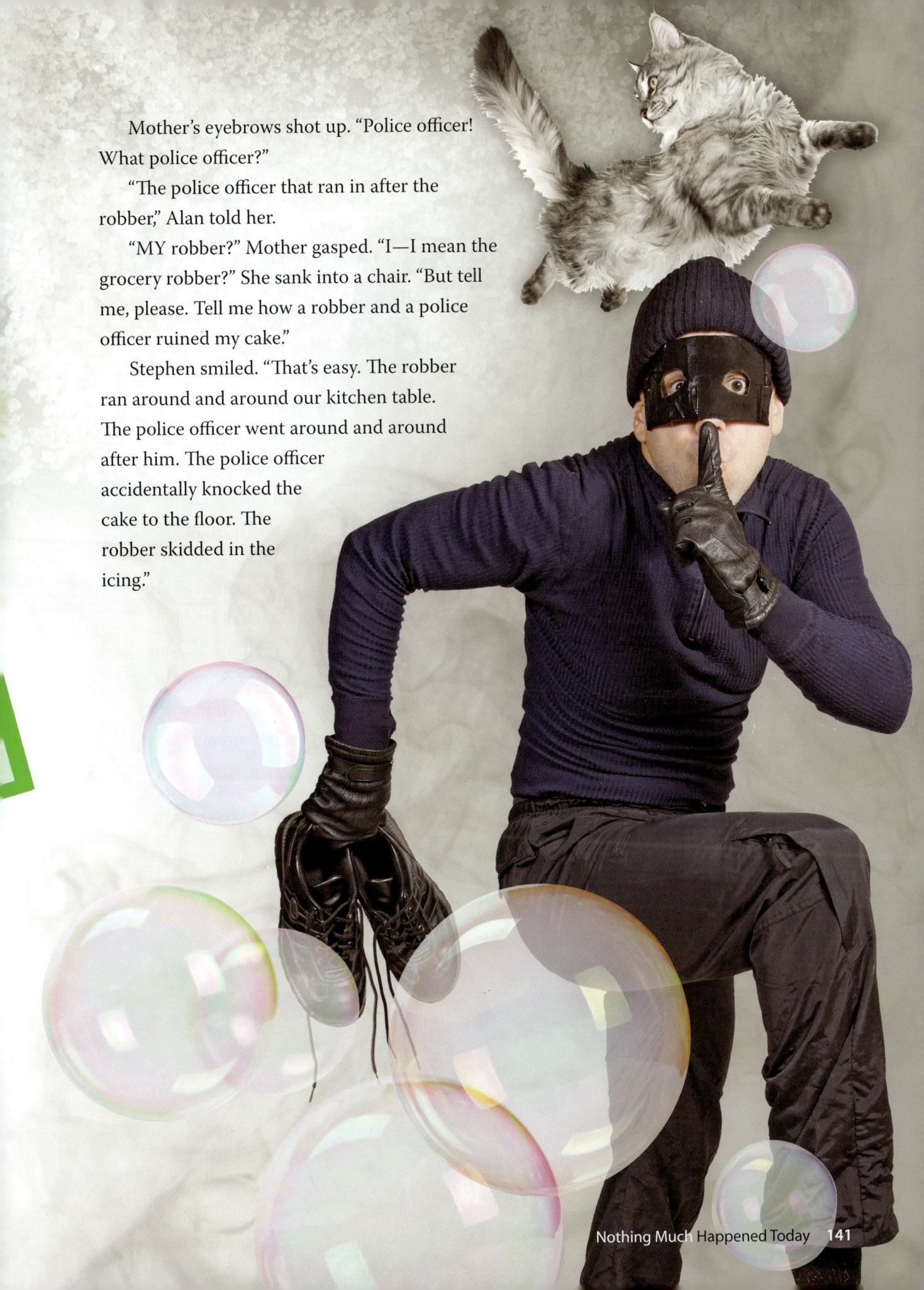

Mother's eyebrows shot up. "Police officer! What police officer?"

"The police officer that ran in after the robber," Alan told her.

"MY robber?" Mother gasped. "I—I mean the grocery robber?" She sank into a chair. "But tell me, please. Tell me how a robber and a police officer ruined my cake."

Stephen smiled. "That's easy. The robber ran around and around our kitchen table. The police officer went around and around after him. The police officer accidentally knocked the cake to the floor. The robber skidded in the icing."

Nothing Much Happened Today 141

Elizabeth interrupted. "And when the robber fell, he hit his head on Alan's head. And you know how hard Alan's head is."

"I know. I know," Mother said. "Let me see now. The robber ran into here and the police officer chased him. They ruined the cake. When you baked a new one you made the oven smokey. Then you opened the window to let the smoke out and the cat came in. Popsicle chased the cat and knocked the sack of sugar on himself. And that's when you bathed him with too many suds?"

"That's right," the three children said together. "And that's when you came home."

"Twenty minutes at the most," Mother said. "I *know* I couldn't have been gone more than twenty minutes, anyway."

"We *told* you nothing much happened today," Stephen said. "How was your day?"

"Nothing much," Mother said, sliding further back into the chair. "Nothing much." The last soap bubble floated gently to the end of her nose where it rested, then popped, and was gone.

About the Author

An only child, **Mary Blount Christian** would tell stories to herself and her imaginary friends and make plays for the neighborhood children. She would roller skate to the library and read her way through the shelves, starting with the As. As an adult, Mrs. Christian has worked as a reporter, writer, and writing teacher for children, college students, and adults. Mrs. Christian has written over 80 children's books. She starts with real experiences and then mixes them with her imagination to create a story. Some of her books have even been translated into Japanese!

I Am Running in a Circle

Jack Prelutsky

I am running in a circle
and my feet are getting sore,
and my head is
spinning
spinning
as it's never spun before,
I am
dizzy
dizzy
dizzy.
Oh! I cannot bear much more,
I am trapped in a revolving
. . . volving
. . . volving
. . . volving door!

Studying the Selection

FIRST IMPRESSIONS
Stephen provided the name for this story. What do you think Mother would have named it?

QUICK REVIEW

1. Where was Mrs. Maeberry when she first noticed the soap bubbles?
2. Why did they have to bathe the dog?
3. What happened to Mother's cake for the bake sale?
4. How long had Mother been gone?

FOCUS

5. How does the title of the story tell us something about Stephen's personality?
6. Draw a small chart on your paper with two columns and three rows. Label one column *cause* and one column *effect*. Under the column labeled *cause*, list three events. Write the effect for each cause on the row next to it in the *effect* column. Here is an example of a cause and its effect:

    cause: the children bathe the dog in soap

    effect: the soap suds make millions of bubbles

CREATING AND WRITING

7. Write two paragraphs about a chain reaction. Use one of the following topic sentences for your beginning:

    The waiter, who was holding a tray of drinks, heard a cry.

    The lights went out in the crowded room.

    Right where the horse was standing, someone set off a firecracker.

8. This story would make a good picture book. Your teacher will divide the class into groups and provide each group with arts and crafts materials. Each group will be assigned to draw one part of the story. Your group will draw a picture of the part assigned to you and write a description of what is happening in the picture at the bottom of the paper. When the groups have completed their pages, your teacher will collect them and bind them into a book.

Nothing Much Happened Today   145

Lesson in Literature...
THE DRIVING TEST

HOW IS SETTING FOR A DRAMA DIFFERENT?

- On a stage the setting is limited to whatever props and scenery are available.
- Often, one or two props will be used to suggest an entire setting. For example, a little sand and an artificial palm tree could be used to suggest a desert.
- Costumes and lighting are very helpful in creating a setting.
- Even background music helps create a setting.

THINK ABOUT IT!

1. In the stage directions for Scene One, several settings are mentioned. Outside the house, the living room, and the kitchen are all listed. If you were performing this play, which room would be the most important one to choose for your setting?
2. Props are a part of setting. List three props that are needed to set the stage for Scene One.
3. What is the setting for Scene Two?

Characters

JESSICA GREEN (age 14)
JEFF GREEN (age 15)
JANET GREEN (their mom, just turned 45)
JILL GREEN (age 8)
BOBBY and SAM GREEN (twins, age 6)
THE BABY
BMV EMPLOYEE
DAVID GREEN (their dad)

Scene One

The home of the Greens. All of the children, except the baby, have just gotten home from school. As usual, Jessica gets the day's mail out of the mailbox as she walks into the house. Jeff is standing in the living room and hangs up his jacket on one of the hooks on the coat rack. As usual, Bobby and Sam drop their jackets on the floor and run into the kitchen for their snack. Jill shouts to them to pick them up. Mom sits at the kitchen table holding the baby.

JESSICA (*looking through the mail*): Hey, everybody! I got a notification from the Bureau of Motor Vehicles that it's time for me to register for my driver's test.

JEFF: That can't be for you. I'm the one who's older. Let me see it. (*He reaches out and grabs the letter out of her hand and pokes her.*)

JESSICA: Mom! It says *J. Green*.

MOM: That was very rude, Jeff. But he's probably right, Jessica. He *is* older. It just can't be helped, my dear. He *did* get here first!

JILL: Well, I guess it couldn't be for *me*. I'm too young! But Jessica, Jeff's name also begins with *J*.

146   Unit 2

JESSICA: Yes, I know. (*She rolls her eyes and looks annoyed.*)

BOBBY: Maybe it's for *us*, me and Sammy. We may be young, but everybody thinks we're cute.

JEFF: Can't be for you two, they don't let you drive just because you're cute, and anyway your names don't begin with *J*.

MOM (*sighing*): Well, I hope it's not for *me*. You know, maybe at 45 they make you take the tests all over again.

JESSICA: Oh Mom, don't be silly. You're not old. (*Jessica gives Mom a hug.*)

BABY: *Wahh-hhh-hhh.*

MOM: Time for me to change the little one!

Scene Two

The next day. At the Bureau of Motor Vehicles. After lots of begging and pleading in the morning with their dad, the children have been given permission to leave school early to go to the BMV to solve the mystery. Which J. Green was the letter for? The line for inquiries is very long. Everyone is growing impatient. Mom even let Jill, Bobby, and Sam come, because they didn't want to be left out. Even Dad shows up. Finally, the eight Greens are at the front of the line.

BMV EMPLOYEE: Next!

(*The Greens step up to the counter.*)

BMV EMPLOYEE: Are all of you here on one matter or let's see, 1-2-3-4-5-6-7 matters? Oops! I didn't count the baby! (*She laughs.*)

THE GREENS (*in one voice*): One matter!

BMV EMPLOYEE: Okay, what's this about?

DAD: Well, we received this notification, but it's not clear whom it's for. It is addressed to *J. Green*. Well, my wife is Janet, my oldest son is Jeff, and my older daughter is Jessica.

BMV EMPLOYEE: Golly, you *all* came in for *that*?

MOM: All the children were very excited about this. How could we leave them home? Besides, it was a family matter.

BMV EMPLOYEE: Let me see. (*She takes the postcard from Dad and types some information into her computer.*)

JEFF (*he elbows his sister, Jessica*): You'll see. Of course it's for me.

JESSICA: Mom! Dad! Will you make him stop poking me?!

MOM: Jeff, this has got to stop!

JEFF: I didn't mean to be mean. Sorry.

BMV EMPLOYEE: Hey, anyone here named Julie Green?

THE GREENS (*in one voice*): *Julie Green*?!

BMV EMPLOYEE: Yeah. You got it. She's the one that's supposed to register for her test.

THE GREENS (*again, in one voice*): But Julie is just a baby!

JESSICA: Mom, show her Julie!

MOM (*holds out the baby, who is sound asleep*): This is the person to whom you sent the notice of registration.

BMV EMPLOYEE: Oh, wow. I'm so sorry for the mistake. And I'm sorry that you Greens had to suffer all of this red tape!

Food's on the Table 147

Blueprint for Reading

INTO... *Food's on the Table*

Six children are looking for an apartment on a lonely street. They arrive and knock on the door. No one is home, so they walk right in. The house is mysteriously empty. Things are not as they expected them to be. Why have their aunt and uncle disappeared? Suddenly, the door opens and ...

Does this sound like a scary mystery? Well, it could have been one, but as it happens, it's a play about some children who make a "delicious" mistake! As you read *Food's on the Table*, ask yourself how you would feel if you were in their shoes.

EYES ON *Drama*

Watching a play is different from reading a book in a number of ways. One way is that instead of having to imagine what the people, places, and objects in the story look like, we see them with our own eyes. Instead of having to imagine how the people in the story sound when they speak, we hear them with our own ears.

When the curtain rises on a play, the first thing the audience sees is the setting of the play. We look at the scenery and we begin to question. Is the setting inside a house? Is the house old-fashioned or modern? Based on what we see on the stage, we make predictions. If the stage is set to look like a palace, we may predict that the play is going to be about royal people in a foreign country. As we watch, we will find out if our predictions are right.

In *Food's on the Table*, the curtains open on a street in old New York, with six children walking along, looking for an address. Although we don't know enough to make many predictions, the setting tells us that we are in a neighborhood where friendly people live. As you read the play, see if this prediction proves to be true.

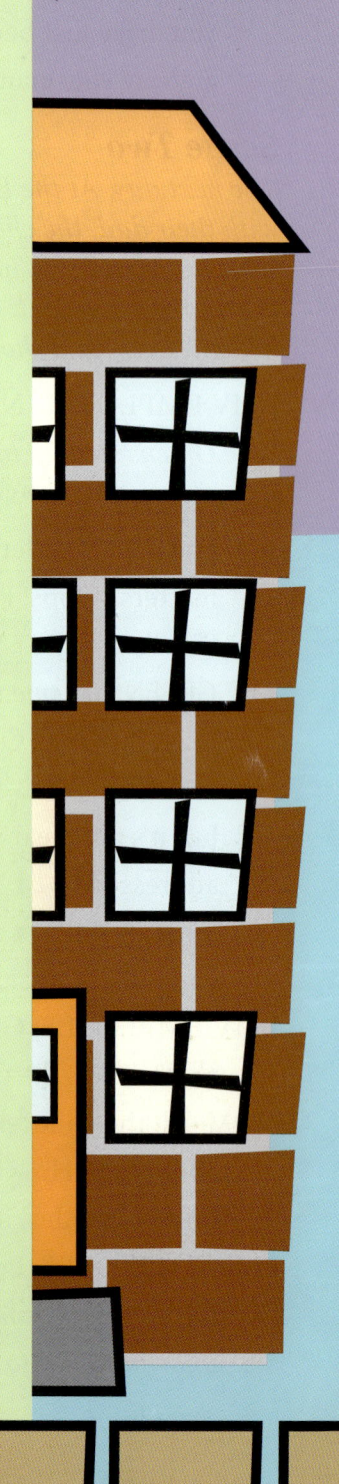

Food's on the Table

adapted from a story by Sydney Taylor

Characters:

ELLA	CHARLIE	MISS BRADY
GERTIE	SARAH	CHARLOTTE
MAMA	HENNY	WOMAN
LENA		

Setting: A city street in New York. The time is 1940.

As Curtain Rises: Children are walking along the street looking for their aunt's apartment.

ELLA: This is the school block, so the house can't be on this one.

CHARLOTTE: What is the number of their building again?

ELLA (*glancing at a slip of paper*): 725. It must be the next block.

(*At right an older woman appears.*)

SARAH: Look! There's my teacher, Miss Brady. It's almost suppertime, and she's just getting out of school.

GERTIE: I thought teachers were only supposed to work till three o'clock.

ELLA: Sometimes there are special things they have to do.

MISS BRADY: Hello, Sarah. What brings you here at this hour?

SARAH (*shyly*): Hello, Miss Brady. Our aunt and uncle just moved to the next block. They want us to see their new apartment, so they invited us for supper.

MISS BRADY: I didn't know you had so many sisters and brothers, Sarah.

SARAH (*grinning*): No, only one brother—little Charlie here. But we're five sisters. This is my oldest sister, Ella. She'll be graduating from high school next year, same time

150   Unit 2

as I graduate from here. Next comes Henny, then me, then Charlotte, and this is Gertie.

MISS BRADY: Quite a family. Are you all as good in history as Sarah?

HENNY: Not me! That's one subject I don't like.

MISS BRADY: Well, this is what I tell my class about that. "You don't like it because you won't like it, and you won't like it because you don't like it." Well, I won't keep you. Good-by and keep studying. (*exits*)

HENNY: History—ugh! Names and places and dates to remember. It's so boring.

SARAH: Oh, but it's not! Not the way Miss Brady teaches anyway. She makes you wish you lived in the olden days.

ELLA: Let's see. 721—723. Here it is—725. It's a nice-looking building. (*glances at paper*) Third floor, apartment 4.

GERTIE: Shouldn't we ring the buzzer?

ELLA: It's out of order. Lena said to go right up.

(*The children climb several flights of stairs and come to apartment number 4.*)

HENNY (*knocking*): There's no answer.

Food's on the Table

ELLA: That's strange. Aunt Lena is expecting us. (*turns doorknob*) Oh, the door is open.

HENNY: She must want us to come right in.

GERTIE: Maybe she's in the bedroom.

ELLA: Lena, Lena. We're here. Lena, Lena?

CHARLOTTE: Is anybody home?

HENNY: Well, anyway, the food's on the table. Mmmm. Homemade corned beef.

GERTIE: And potato salad! And cole slaw! Lena sure knows what we like.

SARAH: Look. She left a note on the table. (*Picking up note, she reads aloud.*) "I had to do some shopping. I'll be a little late. Don't wait for me. Go ahead and eat."

HENNY: Well, that's that. Let's eat.

ELLA: I don't think that would be polite. Let's wait a little while.

SARAH: We could set the table in the meantime. Lena was in an awful hurry. No plates—just three settings of silverware.

HENNY (*opening door to cupboard*): Pretty dishes. Lena must have gotten a new set.

CHARLOTTE: And these kitchen chairs—they are pretty, too.

ELLA: Uncle Hyman must be doing well.

GERTIE: I'm glad Lena has moved near to us. Now we'll be able to see her more often.

CHARLIE: I'm hungry. I want to eat!

ELLA: We have to wait till Lena gets here, Charlie.

CHARLIE: But I'm hungry now.

HENNY: We're all hungry, Charlie. Can't you wait a little longer?

CHARLIE: I'm hunnnngry.

CHARLOTTE: So am I. Couldn't we at least get started? She said to in the note.

ELLA: Well, OK, but there isn't too much dinner, so let's be careful. (*Ella begins to spoon out salad. Children begin to eat.*)

CHARLOTTE: Maybe Lena's not used to cooking for a big mob like us. There are only the two of them.

ELLA: That's true, but you know how they are about food. Usually their table groans with all the food they serve.

CHARLIE: I want another corned beef sandwich.

SARAH: It's a lucky thing corned beef comes in one big piece, or we wouldn't have enough of that, either.

ELLA: Well, take it easy. There's hardly anything left.

(*Suddenly a woman comes in the door carrying a pile of boxes and bags. The children all turn and stare at the stranger.*)

ELLA (*politely*): My aunt isn't here yet.

WOMAN (*puzzled*): You're expecting your aunt?

HENNY: Yes. Don't go away. She'll be here any minute. Let me help you with the packages.

WOMAN: Thank you, but … (*sets down packages*) Now tell me, who are you, anyway?

ELLA: We're the nieces and this is the nephew, Charlie.

WOMAN: That's nice. I'm glad to meet you. (*Looking down at table, a look of dismay crosses her face.*) Oh my goodness! I see you ate up the whole supper!

ELLA: I'm awfully sorry. Were you invited, too?

WOMAN: Who's invited? The supper was for my husband and son.

HENNY: Good gracious. How many people were supposed to eat here tonight?

WOMAN: You don't understand. The supper was just for the three of us—my husband, my son, and me. After all, this *is* my apartment. (*a moment of stunned silence*)

ELLA (*shakily*): Your apartment! This is your apartment?

WOMAN: Yes, darling.

SARAH: But isn't this apartment 4?

WOMAN: Yes.

ELLA: And isn't this the third floor?

WOMAN: No. The third floor is downstairs underneath my apartment. This is the fourth floor.

ELLA (*confused*): But how could that be? We walked up three flights of stairs.

WOMAN (*nodding head*): Oh, I see. You didn't realize that the ground floor is called the first floor. You should have walked up only two flights.

ELLA (*blushing*): What a dreadful mistake. I'm terribly sorry. We thought we were in our aunt's apartment—then we read the note, and …

WOMAN (*chuckling*): Well, what's done is done. Don't worry. A mistake can happen.

HENNY: But we ate up all your food!

WOMAN (*laughing*): Well, as long as you enjoyed it.

(*The children begin to inch their way toward the door.*)

SARAH: We just didn't know—

ELLA: We feel awful about it. And you've been so kind about it.

Food's on the Table   155

(*Mother and Aunt Lena appear at door.*)

MAMA (*demandingly*): What's the matter? Where have you been?

LENA: I was ready to call the police station. I kept opening the door to see if you were coming. Then we heard the voices and we came upstairs to see. What are you doing here?

ELLA: Oh, Mama.

HENNY: We made a mistake.

CHARLOTTE: We thought this was Lena's apartment.

CHARLIE: We ate the corned beef.

MAMA: One at a time. Ella, what happened?

ELLA (*embarrassed*): I know it sounds dreadful, but we went into this lady's apartment and ate her whole supper.

GERTIE: The whole supper. It was supposed to be for her husband and her son.

MAMA: How could you do such a thing? What happened to your manners? How could you sit down and eat with nobody there?

CHARLOTTE: The note said we should.

MAMA: I must apologize for my children. They never did anything like this before.

WOMAN: Don't take it to heart. So they ate a supper in my house. What's wrong with that? Believe me, it was a pleasure to see so many nice young faces around my table.

MAMA: It was very wrong of them. They had no right—

LENA (*placing hand on mama's arm and laughing loudly*): Oh, you children. You ate up the lady's supper. Oh, Mama, they ate up the whole supper. Don't you see how funny it is? Oh! Oh! Oh!

(*Everyone begins to laugh.*)

WOMAN (*laughing*): Next—time— (*laughter*) next time—children, let me know—when you're coming—so I'll prepare enough.

LENA: Well, neighbor, what is your name?

WOMAN: It's Mrs. Shiner. Molly Shiner.

LENA: This certainly is a comical way for us to meet. Listen, Mrs. Shiner. I have plenty of food downstairs. Enough for twenty people! Leave another note on your table for your husband and son, and come downstairs with us. Everyone is invited for supper!

About the Author

Sydney Taylor grew up in a Jewish family in a crowded apartment on the Lower East Side of New York. Mrs. Taylor would tell her daughter, Joanne, bedtime stories about her fond memories sharing a small bedroom with four sisters. Mrs. Taylor wrote these stories down for her daughter, and as a surprise, her husband submitted them to a contest. The publishers running the contest liked Mrs. Taylor's book so much that they wanted to publish it! Children loved *All-of-a-Kind Family*, and its publication began Mrs. Taylor's writing career.

BREAKFAST Jeff Moss

I C U 8 your scrambled X,

I C U drank your T.

My heart is filled with NV,

R there NE X 4 me?

O Y is the carton MT now?

How greedy can U B?

4 U 8 all the scrambled X

And left me 1 green P!

Studying the Selection

FIRST IMPRESSIONS
Have you ever had the feeling that something was not quite right, but couldn't figure out what it was?

QUICK REVIEW

1. For what were the children searching?
2. Why had they been invited to their aunt's and uncle's apartment?
3. What made them think the supper was for them?
4. What did Aunt Lena do at the end to make everyone feel good?

FOCUS

5. The children thought they were on the third floor, but they were on the fourth. Explain how they made this mistake.
6. There were a number of clues that told the children they were in the wrong apartment. What were three of those clues?

CREATING AND WRITING

7. In *Food's on the Table*, there are "facts" that could mean one thing, but really mean another. Your teacher is now going to read a story to you. The meaning of the story is not clear because the details can be explained in more than one way. Write a paragraph that gives your explanation of the story and makes everything clear. Then, since the story stops in the middle, write a good ending for it.
8. This play is about a family of children who make a big mistake. Your teacher will divide the class into groups. Each group will make a short play based on a mistake someone has made and present it to the class. Curtains up!

Lesson in Literature...
CROSSING AMERICA

WHAT IS THE MAIN IDEA?

- A story, play, poem, or an essay must all have a **main idea**.
- The less important (minor) ideas in the story should be connected to the main idea.
- In a well-written story, the characters, plot, and setting all contribute to the main idea.
- To discover the story's main idea, ask yourself: What is this story *about*?

THINK ABOUT IT!

1. The story's setting is very important to the main idea. What is the story's setting?
2. What are two less important ideas in the story that are linked to the main idea?
3. What is the main idea of this story?

We reached Vermillion Creek in the late afternoon and set up camp. There were the good smells of food cooking. Nothing special to eat but beans and bread and coffee, but it's nice to stop and rest and chat a little.

We are twenty wagons, and we are only at the beginning of our long journey. We just crossed the Missouri River. My Mama said we were seeing "the last of civilization." It has been hard to say goodbye to everything: my teacher, our fancy dresses, my best friend Emilia, and my pretty bedroom.

No one really knows what is ahead. We were told that when people first started crossing the Overland Trail they had bad maps. There were no settlers along the way to help them if they needed supplies. It is better now, Pa says, but it is hardly like living as we used to, in a city with shops and schools and neighbors. We sort of knew what to expect each day.

My Mama says that she, like many of the other women, really does not want to make this hard journey. She doesn't want to scare me, but she says it is important for me to know how difficult it will be. Yes, it will be an adventure. And if we all get there healthy, safe, and sound, and live in a good community, it will have been worth it. But I need to prepare myself to be very strong. Then she reminds me that I am only eight, and I'm still a young girl, so I can still come to her and complain!

Although the guidebooks say the trip takes three to four months, I know it is more like six to eight months. That means there will be some really bad weather. I know Mama will have a baby along the way. That will be very hard on her. I hope I can be a really big help to her.

Mama is not as afraid of the Indians as Pa is. She says that the Indians we have met were helpful. Pa calls them savages, even if they speak our language or are nice to us. Mama says they have made some good food trades with us, like those potatoes that we needed so badly. Pa just doesn't agree with that nice talk. Maybe he feels that way because getting along with Indians is new to him.

My Pa is a big man, tall and very strong, and stern. Actually, I don't call Pa, Pa. I call him Sir. He says no matter what, we have to get that free land in Oregon.

My Ma and all the other women and girls do all of the chores on the trail: They fix meals and sew; wash, dry, fold, and mend clothes; and care for the children. They figure out how to pack up the wagons. They drive the ox teams and collect buffalo chips as fuel for fires when there is no wood.

I don't know how the women and girls get it all done. The women on the trail also do all the caretaking of the sick or the injured or the dying. There have been times when epidemics of cholera have swept over the wagons of people going west. So far we have been spared.

We older children have been warned repeatedly that little children and even babies fall out of wagons. Children wander off and get lost. They can get lost with all the people, goats, and oxen milling around. Therefore, we are organizing teams to look out for the little ones.

Last night it poured. There was a huge rainstorm. Our wagons and tents were overturned. Mama, Pa, and I just tried to curl up and sleep. But all through the night we were wet, muddy, and cold. Today, the sun is shining and our clothes are drying out. On the road, we move through a forest that is so thick you almost can't see the sky. Pa says the trees are 300 feet high. Wow!

There's not a lot of time to write. Mama likes to write a little bit each day, too. I think it gives us a sense of security, when so much is happening that is new.

Blueprint for Reading

INTO . . . *Across the Wide Dark Sea*

Walk out into the street of any city in America. Horns are honking, buses are rumbling. Buildings, lights, signs, and people are everywhere you look. It's crowded and noisy and full of life. Now close your eyes and imagine these same cities when the first settlers came from Europe to America. Where there are streets and cars today, there are forests and wild animals. Any food or clothing or tools that you have were brought with you on a ship from the old country. If you want a house, you will have to build one. If you want vegetables, you will have to grow them. There is illness, cold, and Indians. But there is something else. There is the good, rich land. There is freedom to make a good life here. And there is your father's firm hand on your shoulder, telling you this is the place you want to be.

EYES ON *Main Idea*

In your imagination, picture a tree. It has a trunk and some branches. The branches have twigs and the twigs have leaves. A story is something like that. It has a **main idea** that can be compared to the tree trunk. Branching off of the main idea are some smaller ideas. These are connected to the main idea and help explain it. A story has many details, such as names and descriptions of how things look. These are like the twigs and leaves on the branches. Although they are important, they are not nearly as important as the main idea. When you read a story, you should be thinking about the following question: What is the author saying? Make sure you don't mistake a smaller idea or a detail for the main idea of the story.

As you read *Across the Wide Dark Sea*, try to identify the story's main idea, and then see if you can identify some of the smaller ideas and details, too.

162   Unit 2

Across the Wide Dark Sea
The Mayflower Journey

Jean Van Leeuwen

I stood close to my father as the anchor was pulled dripping from the sea. Above us, white sails rose against a bright blue sky. They fluttered, then filled with wind. Our ship began to move.

My father was waving to friends on shore. I looked back at their faces growing smaller and smaller, and ahead at the wide dark sea. And I clung to my father's hand.

We were off on a journey to an unknown land.

The ship was packed tight with people—near a hundred, my father said. We were crowded below deck in a space so low that my father could barely stand upright, and so cramped that we could scarcely stretch out to sleep.

Packed in tight, too, was everything we would need in the new land: tools for building and planting, goods for trading, guns for hunting. Food, furniture, clothing, books. A few crates of chickens, two dogs, and a striped orange cat.

> **WORD BANK**
> **scarcely** (SKAIRS lee)
> *adv.*: hardly

Our family was luckier than most. We had a corner out of the damp and cold. Some had to sleep in the ship's small work boat.

The first days were fair, with a stiff wind.

My mother and brother were seasick down below. But I stood on deck and watched the sailors hauling on ropes, climbing in the rigging, and perched at the very top of the mast, looking out to sea.

What a fine life it must be, I thought, to be a sailor.

> **WORD BANK**
>
> **hauling** (HAWL ing)
> *v.*: pulling

Across the Wide Dark Sea

One day clouds piled up in the sky. Birds with black wings circled the ship, and the choppy sea seemed angry.

"Storm's cooking," I heard a sailor say. We were all sent below as the sailors raced to furl the sails.[1]

Then the storm broke. Wind howled and waves crashed. The ship shuddered as it rose and fell in seas as high as mountains. Some people were crying, others praying. I huddled next to my father, afraid in the dark.

How could a ship so small and helpless ever cross the vast ocean?

The sun came out. We walked on deck and dried our clothes. But just when my shoes felt dry at last, more clouds gathered.

"Storm's coming," I told my father.

So the days passed, each one like the last. There was nothing to do but eat our meals of salt pork, beans, and bread, tidy up our cramped space, sleep when we could, and try to keep dry. When it was not too stormy we climbed on deck to stretch our legs.

---

1. During a storm, the sails on a ship are *furled*, rolled up and tied to the mast, to keep the wind from blowing the ship off course, or tipping it over.

> **WORD BANK**
>
> **vast** *adj.*: huge; covering a very great area

But even then we had to keep out of the sailors' way.

How I longed to run and jump and climb!

Once during a storm a man was swept overboard. Reaching out with desperate hands, he caught hold of a rope and clung to it.

Down he went under the raging foaming water.

Then, miraculously, up he came.

Sailors rushed to the side of the ship. Hauling on the rope, they brought him in close and with a boat hook plucked him out of the sea. And his life was saved.

WORD BANK
desperate (DESS prit) *adj.*: extremely needy
raging (RAY jing) *adj.*: angry and dangerous
miraculously (mih RAK yuh luss lee) *adv.*: as though through a miracle
plucked *v.*: pulled out with force

Across the Wide Dark Sea

Storm followed storm. The pounding of wind and waves caused one of the main beams to crack, and our ship began to leak.

Worried, the men gathered in the captain's cabin to talk of what to do. Could our ship survive another storm? Or must we turn back?

They talked for two days, but could not agree.

Then someone thought of the iron jack[2] for raising houses that they were taking to the new land.

---

2. A *jack* is a tool used to lift heavy objects. (Most cars carry jacks in their trunks so that the car can be raised if a tire needs changing.)

Word Bank

beams *n.*: thick, strong boards that go across the width of a ship

168 Unit 2

Using it to lift the cracked beam, the sailors set a new post underneath, tight and firm, and patched all the leaks.

And our ship sailed on.

For six weeks we had traveled, and still there was no land in sight. Now we were always cold and wet. Water seeping in from above put out my mother's cooking fire, and there was nothing to eat but hard dry biscuits and cheese. My brother was sick, and many others too.

And some began to ask why we had left our safe homes to go on this endless journey to an unknown land.

Why? I also asked the question of my father that night.

"We are searching for a place to live where we can worship G-d in our own way," he said quietly. "It is this freedom we seek in a new land. And I have faith that we will find it."

Looking at my father, so calm and sure, suddenly I too had faith that we would find it.

Across the Wide Dark Sea

Still the wide dark sea went on and on. Eight weeks. Nine.

Then one day a sailor, sniffing the air, said, "Land's ahead." We dared not believe him. But soon bits of seaweed floated by. Then a tree branch. And a feather from a land bird.

Two days later at dawn I heard the lookout shout, "Land ho!"

Everyone who was well enough to stand crowded on deck. And there through the gray mist we saw it: a low dark outline between sea and sky. Land!

Tears streamed down my mother's face, yet she was smiling. Then everyone fell to their knees while my father said a prayer of thanksgiving.

Our long journey was over.

The ship dropped anchor in a quiet bay, circled by land. Pale yellow sand and dark hunched trees were all we saw. And all we heard was silence.

What lurked among those trees? Wild beasts? Wild men? Would there be food and water, a place to take shelter?

What waited for us in this new land?

A small party of men in a small boat set off to find out. All day I watched on deck for their return.

When at last they rowed into sight, they brought armfuls of firewood and tales of what they had seen: forests of fine trees, rolling hills of sand, swamps and ponds and rich black earth. But no houses or wild beasts or wild men.

So all of us went ashore.

My mother washed the clothes we had worn for weeks beside a shallow pond, while my brother and I raced up and down the beach.

We watched whales spouting in the sparkling blue bay and helped search for firewood. And we found clams and mussels, the first fresh food we had tasted in two months. I ate so many I was sick.

Day after day the small party set out from the ship, looking for just the right place to build our settlement.

> **WORD BANK**
>
> **settlement** (SET ul ment) *n.*: the beginnings of a town; a group of houses built in a new, unsettled area

172 Unit 2

The days grew cold. Snowflakes danced in the wind. The cold and damp made many sick again. Drawing his coat tightly around him, my father looked worried.

"We must find a place," he said, "before winter comes."

One afternoon the weary men returned with good news. They had found the right spot at last.

When my father saw it, he smiled. It was high on a hill, with a safe harbor and fields cleared for planting and brooks running with sweet water. We named it after the town from which we had sailed, across the sea.

It was December now, icy cold and stormy. The men went ashore to build houses, while the rest of us stayed on board ship. Every fine day they worked. But as the houses of our settlement began to rise, more and more of our people fell sick. And some of them died.

It was a long and terrible winter.

We had houses now, small and rough. Yet the storms and sickness went on. And outside the settlement, Indians waited, seldom seen but watching us.

My father and mother nursed the sick, and my father led prayers for them. But more and more died. Of all the people who had sailed for the new land, only half were left.

One morning in March, as I was gathering firewood, I heard a strange sweet sound. Looking up, I saw birds singing in a white birch tree.

Could it be that spring had come at last?

All that day the sun shone warm, melting the snow. The sick rose from their beds. And once more the sound of axes and the smell of new-split wood filled the air.

"We have done it," my father said. "We have survived the winter."

But now the Indians came closer. We found their arrows, and traces of their old houses. We caught sight of them among the trees. Our men met to talk of this new danger. How could so small a settlement defend itself?

Cannons were mounted on top of the hill, and the men took turns standing guard. Then one day an Indian walked into the settlement. Speaking to us in our own language, he said, "Welcome."

Our Indian friend came back and brought his chief. We all agreed to live in peace.

And one of the Indians stayed with us, teaching us where to find fish in the bubbling brooks, and how to catch them in traps, and how to plant Indian corn so that next winter we would have enough to eat.

My father and I worked side by side, clearing the fields, planting barley and peas and hills of corn.

Afterward I dug a garden next to our house. In it we planted the seeds we had brought from home: carrots and cabbages and onions and my mother's favorite herbs, parsley, sage, chamomile, and mint.

Each day I watched, until something green pushed up from the dark earth. My mother laughed when she saw it.

"Perhaps we may yet make a home in this new land," she said.

On a morning early in April our ship sailed back across the sea. We gathered on shore to watch it go. The great white sails filled with wind, then slowly the ship turned and headed out into the wide dark sea.

I watched it growing smaller and smaller, and suddenly there were tears in my eyes. We were all alone now.

Then I felt a hand on my shoulder.

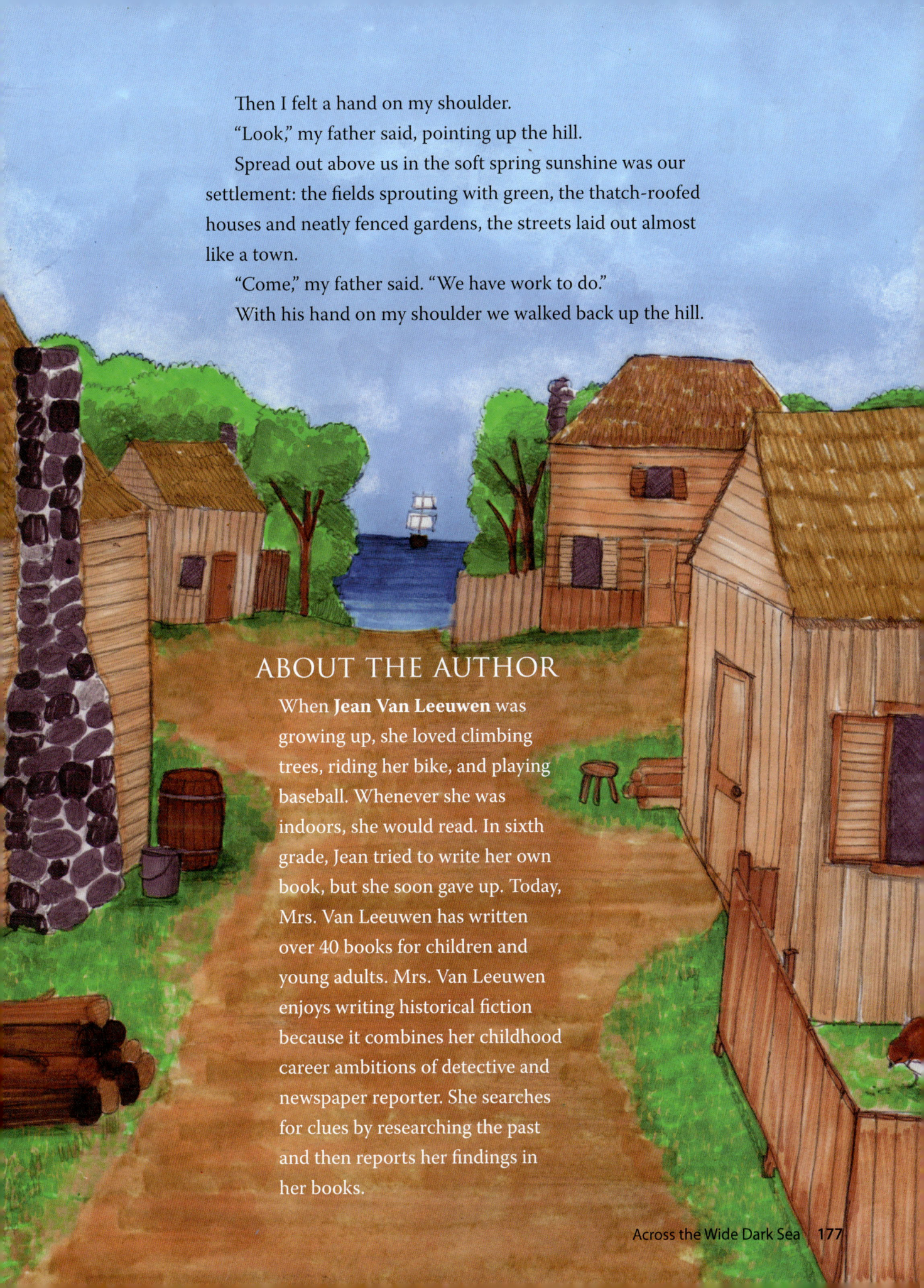

"Look," my father said, pointing up the hill.

Spread out above us in the soft spring sunshine was our settlement: the fields sprouting with green, the thatch-roofed houses and neatly fenced gardens, the streets laid out almost like a town.

"Come," my father said. "We have work to do."

With his hand on my shoulder we walked back up the hill.

ABOUT THE AUTHOR

When **Jean Van Leeuwen** was growing up, she loved climbing trees, riding her bike, and playing baseball. Whenever she was indoors, she would read. In sixth grade, Jean tried to write her own book, but she soon gave up. Today, Mrs. Van Leeuwen has written over 40 books for children and young adults. Mrs. Van Leeuwen enjoys writing historical fiction because it combines her childhood career ambitions of detective and newspaper reporter. She searches for clues by researching the past and then reports her findings in her books.

Across the Wide Dark Sea 177

The World with Its Countries

John Cotton

The world with its countries,
Mountains and seas,
People and creatures,
Flowers and trees,
The fish in the waters,
The birds in the air
Are calling to ask us
All to take care.

These are our treasures,
A gift from above,
We should say thank you
With a care that shows love
For the blue of the ocean,
The clearness of air,
The wonder of forests
And the valleys so fair.

The song of the skylark,
The warmth of the sun,
The rushing of clear streams
And new life begun
Are gifts we should cherish,
So join in the call
To strive to preserve them
For the future of all.

Studying the Selection

FIRST IMPRESSIONS
If you were going to a new land, would you be excited or frightened?

QUICK REVIEW

1. Describe the conditions on the ship.
2. When the boy asked his father why they were going to a new land, what did his father answer?
3. About how many weeks had passed when they reached the new land?
4. When the group of men went to look over the new land, what did they report?

FOCUS

5. Why didn't the people all get off the ship as soon as they reached land?
6. Why did the boy's mother laugh when she saw the vegetables growing in her garden?

CREATING AND WRITING

7. Many people who journeyed to America kept a journal of their travels. Imagine that you were on the ship described in this story. Write four journal entries. The first should be for the day the ship set sail; the second should be for the day of the storm; the third should be the day you saw land; and the fourth should be in the springtime when the crops were beginning to grow.

8. The people on the ship had to bring along everything they would need to start their new lives. This included (a) clothing (b) building materials and tools (c) seeds and gardening tools and (d) food that could be used on the journey. Your teacher will divide your class into groups. Each group will "pack" what would be needed for one of these categories. Think about what would be absolutely necessary and make a list of what you will pack. Put these items (or pictures of them) into a suitcase, box, or bag and present them to your class, explaining why you packed each item. Remember two things: First, there is very little room on the ship so you can bring only what you need. Second, whatever you bring must be able to survive the trip.

Across the Wide Dark Sea

Jill's Journal:
On Assignment on the Mayflower

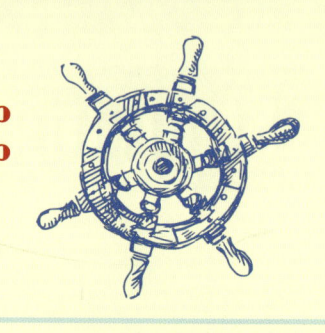

What do you think it would be like to cross the Atlantic Ocean on a very small ship? Imagine doing this with more than 100 other passengers, all of their belongings, and some farm animals. This does not include the crew, the officers, and the master of the ship!

Well, it's 1620, and you may remember that I am Jill, Investigative Reporter, and that I travel back and forth in time. I am going to be staying with the Pilgrims, on board, for the entire journey—that's 66 days in a dark, cramped space with no lights or windows! I figured that if the Pilgrims could make it on the *Mayflower*, then so could I. Now I'm not so sure.

This is history that you can find in books. I read about it before I decided to make the voyage, so I shouldn't worry so. But I am feeling very nervous as the *Mayflower* sets sail from Plymouth Harbor, England. We have missed traveling in fair weather. I know that the voyage is going to take much longer than anyone thought.

What I am learning as we sail is that it is different to read about something than to have it happen to you. For example, events don't make me seasick if I am just reading about them, but when the ship comes crashing down from the top of a wave, I feel really sick.

I hear from the other passengers and the crew that pirates attack ships. They say that they have to be on the lookout for pirates all the time. I worry about this a lot, even though I *know* no pirates attacked the *Mayflower*. Remember, I've traveled back in time, and I really know what happened on this trip.

The autumn is a stormy time at sea. The storms frighten all of us and many get very sick from the rough movement of the water against the ship. Also, when it is stormy and the waves are huge, we cannot go up on deck and get fresh air. None of us has had a bath for several weeks. You can imagine that this is a place you might not want to be.

Forgive me for complaining so much, but I even find it hard to write in my journal. There is *so* little light down here, and we keep being knocked about by the ship's movement. (You should try writing with the feathers they use for pens!) However, my journal is the only thing that keeps my mind off of the difficulties. I try to be helpful to some of the mothers who aren't well, so that I will stop thinking constantly about myself. How can I be describing what the *Mayflower* voyage was like, if all I am doing is suffering?

I have just learned that the most recent storm is over, but it has cracked one of the big wooden beams. I'm pleased the crew has fixed it with something called a "great iron screw." I am not really interested in exactly how they fixed the ship, just as long as it's fixed and we get to America and I can go home!

I haven't written in my journal for more than a week now. But today, events were so exciting that I have forced myself to take pen to paper. We had just been through another bad storm. During the storm, John Howland—one of the passengers—was swept off the deck of the ship! How horrible! He must have been so frightened! But Mr. Howland is very quick-thinking and he grabbed onto one of the ship's ropes that was hanging in the sea. The sailors pulled him back on the deck. We have something to celebrate!

As the weeks have passed, everyone has been safe. All those who were sick have recovered, except for one sailor. We have been blessed by the birth of a baby during the journey. Elizabeth Hopkins has named her son, Oceanus! This is her and her husband's second child. Their little girl is also on board.

Finally, the day has arrived. After more than two months at sea, we reached Cape Cod on November 11th. The group will sail up the coast to Plymouth and begin constructing their town.

I will be leaving shortly. This has been a hard trip. I do not envy these dear people the winter that is almost upon them. It gets very cold here. I feel love for many of my fellow passengers. Remember, I have time-traveled from the future, and I know what is going to happen. I know that many of the people I have come to know so well will die this first winter. In a little bit less than a year, in 1621, those settlers who remain will have a feast to give thanks for coming through the voyage and the first winter.

POWER SKILL:
Learning to Write About the Past

1. When writing a story that takes place long ago, an author has to be careful not to include objects that did not exist at that time. For example, if a writer described Abraham Lincoln turning on his radio to hear the news, the reader would laugh. The radio had not yet been invented when Abraham Lincoln was alive! In your notebook, make two columns. At the top of the first, write *Mayflower*, and at the top of the second, write *Modern*. Look at the list of objects below and put each of them into one of the columns.

Potatoes	Seeds for wheat
Blender	Captain's spyglass
Light bulbs	Down quilts
Spades	Electric blankets
Washing soap	A box of Cheerios
Calculator	Books

2. It's your turn to write a page in a journal. You are writing in the cabin that you and your fellow Pilgrims built after landing in Plymouth. Write about details such as what you're sitting on, what you're writing on, and what you're eating.

3. Draw a picture of the inside of the cabin.

Jill's Journal

unit 2 wrap-up

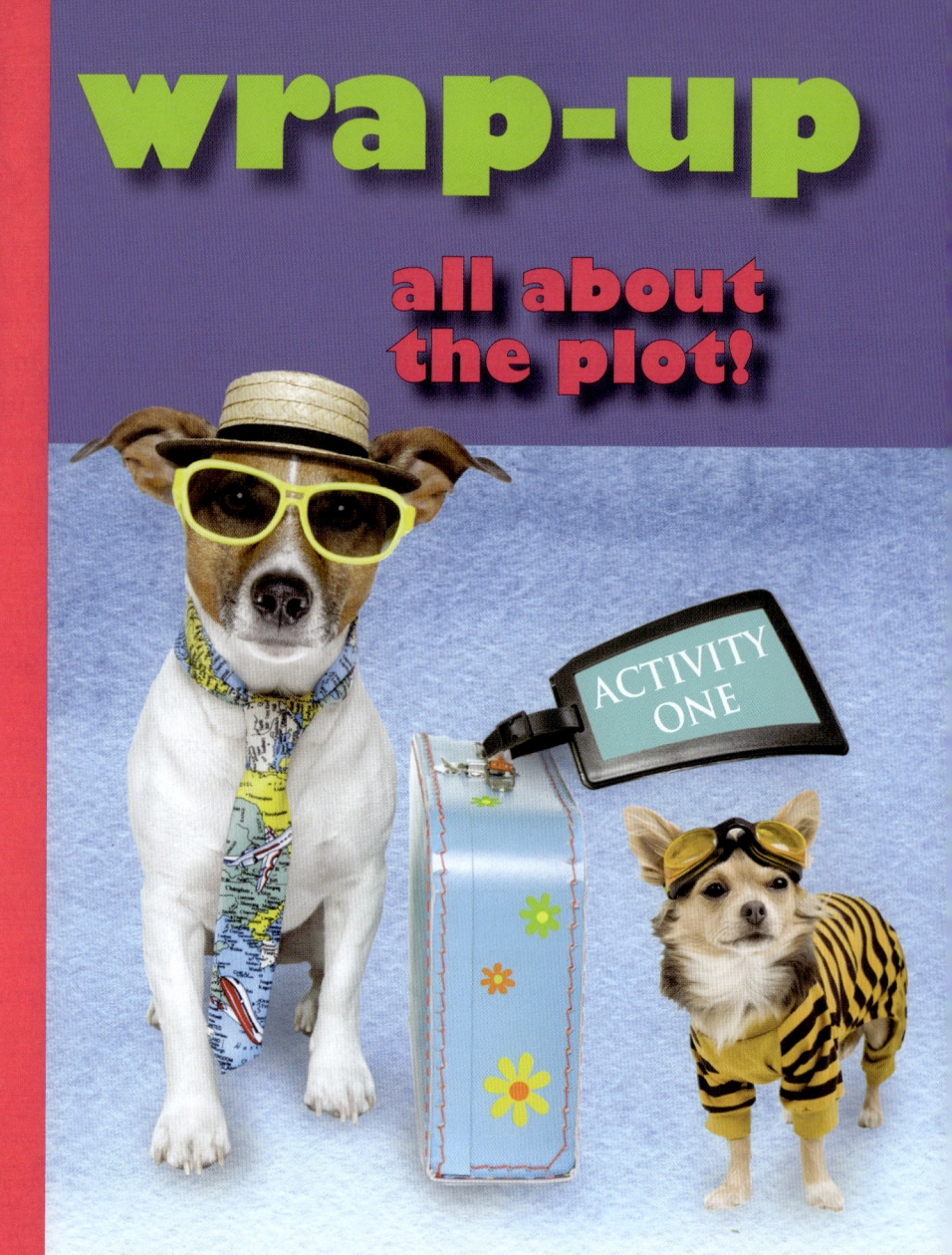

all about the plot!

ACTIVITY ONE

In three of the stories in Unit Two, the main character travels from one place to another. A young boy sails on a ship from Europe to America in *Across the Wide Dark Sea*, Sybil rides her horse all through the Connecticut countryside in *Sybil Rides By Night*, and Jangmi flies on an airplane to America in *Good-Bye, 382 Shin Dang Dong*. In each story, the reader learns what the ride was like and how the character felt when the journey was over.

For the following exercise, choose one of the three main characters named in the paragraph above. Your teacher will provide you with two sheets of paper and some crayons or markers. One sheet of paper will be lined for writing. On it, you will write a six-line poem that doesn't rhyme. We have provided you with the first

Good-Bye, 382 Shin Dang Dong

Sybil Rides By Night

Nothing Much Happened Today

Food's on the Table

Across the Wide Dark Sea

two lines of the poem. Copy it onto the lined paper, and then write two lines which describe the character's journey. Write two more lines that describe how the character felt when the journey was over. You will now have a six-line poem. Take the crayons and the sheet of paper and draw a picture of your character on his or her journey.

Here are the first two lines for each of the poems:

1.

For the narrator of *Across the Wide Dark Sea*:

I sailed on a ship
Across the wide, dark sea

2.

For Sybil from *Sybil Rides By Night*:

I rode on a horse
Up and down the hills

3.

For Jangmi from *Good-Bye, 382 Shin Dang Dong*:

I flew on a plane
To a land that was strange and new

Unit 2 Wrap-Up

unit 2 wrap-up continued

ACTIVITY TWO

Each of the selections in this unit takes place in a different place and at a different time. Choose a character from any one of the selections who is *not* a main character. With costumes provided by your teacher or brought from home, dress up as that character. Write a short paragraph about yourself and prepare to present it to the class.

Here's an example. You have chosen to be a sailor on board the ship in *Across the Wide Dark Sea*. Dress up as a sailor and prepare a little speech telling the class what your name is, what country you were born in, and what the life of a sailor is like.

ACTIVITY THREE

Although only one of the Unit Two selections is a drama, all of the selections could be *dramatized*, which means turned into a play. Your teacher will divide your class into five groups. Each group will be given one of the selections to dramatize. Each group should do the following:

1. Choose one scene of the story or play that you think is the most interesting.
2. Assign a part to each member of the group. If there are not enough parts, you may make up a character and some lines. For example, you could give Jangmi another friend or relative.
3. It's always fun to have some kind of costume or prop. Even a hat or scarf can be a costume. See what you can use to add some interest to your drama.
4. Decide what each actor is going to say.
5. Rehearse your scene.
6. Have a narrator tell the class what has happened in the play up until the part you are presenting.
7. Present the scene to the class.

ACTIVITY FOUR

Two of the selections in Unit Two are humorous. They are *Nothing Much Happened Today* and *Food's on the Table*. Are you a good comic writer? Let's see! Choose one of these selections and go over it in your mind. Then, think up a different ending for the story you chose, and write your idea down. Make sure your ending includes at least one new, exciting event that makes the story turn out differently. If you are writing an ending for *Food's on the Table*, don't forget to write your ending as a play.

Unit 2 Wrap-Up

unit 3

THOUGHTFUL

BRAVE

BORED

CONCERN

STUBBORN

all about characters!

Lesson in Literature...
A Different Kind of Hero

WHAT ARE CHARACTER TRAITS?

- **Character traits** determine the way a person thinks, feels, and behaves. Examples of character traits are honesty and dishonesty; generosity and stinginess; patience and impatience. Notice that character traits can be good or bad.
- You cannot always see a character trait, but you can feel one. You cannot always *see* whether a person is kind or cruel, but you can *feel* it.
- In real life, a person has many character traits.
- In a story, a character may appear to have only a few character traits. This is because the author wishes to focus on those few.

THINK ABOUT IT!

1. The mother had the character trait of kindness. What is one example of the mother's kindness?
2. The mother had the character trait of generosity. What is one example of the mother's generosity?
3. The mother had a third character trait. It was her ability to sense how a person was feeling and do something about it. If a person was feeling lonely, she might strike up a conversation. What example of the mother's sensitivity to another person's feelings can you find in the story?

When I was growing up, my father, my mother, my sister, and I lived in a house in Newark, New Jersey. It was not a big house, and the neighborhood was not a fancy one. But inside our house, we had many beautiful things and two grand pianos.

My mother loved to collect antiques. She was also a very good pianist and a fine piano teacher with many students. When I think about her these days, however, those are not the pictures that I see in my mind. Even though my mother had a great love of music and art, she was a person who never forgot those in need. Extra money was used first for those who needed it more than we did.

If I could write a letter to her today, I would say: *Dear Mommy: What I remember most about you is being loved by you. I loved knowing that you cared not just about us, but that you worried about people or animals who did not have enough.*

When my parents were able to afford cleaning help, they hired an older woman who was sickly. She was not very strong, so my mother cleaned right beside her, especially taking on the heavier, harder tasks. My sister asked my mom why she bothered to have a cleaning lady. My mother said, "Sarah comes because she needs the job." If there was a time when Sarah couldn't come—let's say she was sick—my mom still paid her for the day.

I remember that my mom had been saving to buy a lovely old pitcher. Then she learned of a family with four children and a baby that had no place to stay. On our second floor, we had an extra bedroom with an attached kitchen. That is where the seven of them lived for several months. We all shared one bathroom. The day before the family arrived, my mom filled up their refrigerator with food. She never did buy that lovely old pitcher, for she had used the money for the family.

I recall a homeless person knocking on our front door looking for a meal. My mother set a little table for him on the front porch with a tablecloth and a cloth napkin. She made him a delicious sandwich, and gave him a glass of iced tea with an orange and a slice of cake. I had never seen anyone do that before. I have never seen anyone else do that to this day. When he left, he carried a bag with fruit, a loaf of bread, some cheese, some cookies, and a clean shirt.

There are different kinds of heroes. A person can save a spirit. My mother's heroic deeds were her kindnesses. She showed me how to pay attention to the lives of other people. Now my daughters show their children. Kindness starts with a little seed and grows into a tall and wondrous tree.

Blueprint for Reading

INTO . . . *The Printer*

The Printer is based on a true story. A boy tells of his deaf father who works in a big building with a lot of other printers. Some of them are deaf, and others can hear. The hearing workers do not bother to talk to the deaf printers. However, the other deaf workers are his friends and they "talk" to each other in sign language. One day, something happens and all the printers have to be warned to leave the building. The warnings are drowned out by the noise of the big printing presses. Can anyone save these men? As you read *The Printer*, think about what advantages a deaf person might have in a noisy environment. Ask yourself, too, if the hearing printers had a lesson to learn.

EYES ON *Character Attributes*

Studying a character in a book or story is like putting together the pieces of a puzzle. We take all the information given to us by the author and piece together a picture. From the character's actions, words, and thoughts, we try to understand what sort of person the character is.

As you read *The Printer*, look for pieces of information that will help you understand the father. What makes him smile or frown? How does he feel about his son? How does his son feel about him? How does he react to danger? Readers love to get to know the characters about whom they are reading. It's almost like having a new friend!

The Printer

Myron Uhlberg

My father was a printer. He wore a printer's four-cornered newspaper hat. Every day after work, he brought home the next day's paper. After reading it, he always folded a page into a small hat and gently placed it on my head.

I would not take off my newspaper hat until bedtime.

My father was deaf. Though he could not hear, he felt through the soles of his shoes the pounding and rumbling of the giant printing presses that daily spat out the newspaper he helped create.

As a boy, my father learned how to speak with his hands. As a man, he learned how to turn lead-type letters[1] into words and sentences. My father loved being a printer.

Sometimes my father felt sad about the way he was treated by his fellow workers who could hear. Because they couldn't talk to him with their hands, they seemed to ignore him. Years went by as my father and the hearing printers worked side by side. They never once exchanged a single thought.

---

1. A printing press has wood or metal blocks with raised letters. The letters are placed so that they form words. Ink is put onto these raised *lead-type letters*, and the letters are pressed onto paper. This is how something is printed.

WORD BANK
exchanged (ex CHANGED) *v.*: traded

But my father did not lack friends. There were other printers at the plant who were deaf. They had also learned to talk with their hands.

One day, while the giant presses ran, their noises shutting out all other sound, my father spotted a fire flickering in a far corner of the pressroom.

The fire was spreading quickly, silently. Suddenly, the wood floor burst into flames.

My father knew he had to tell everyone. He couldn't speak to shout a warning. Even if he could, no one would hear him over the load roar of the presses.

But he could speak with his hands.

He did not hesitate. He jumped onto an ink drum and waved his arms excitedly until, clear across the room, he caught the attention of a fellow printer who also couldn't hear a sound.

My father's hands shouted through the terrible noise of the printing presses,
FIRE! FIRE!
TELL EVERYONE TO GET OUT!
TELL THE HEARING ONES!
His friend climbed onto a huge roll of newsprint. His fingers screamed to the other deaf workers,
FIRE! FIRE!
TELL THE HEARING ONES!
All the printers who couldn't hear ran to fellow workers who could. They pointed to the fire, which had now spread to the wall next to the only exit.

Not one of my father's friends left until everyone knew of the danger. My father was the last to escape.

FIRE

The Printer 195

By the time everyone had fled, the fire—feeding on huge quantities of paper—had engulfed the enormous plant. The giant presses, some still spewing out burning sheets of newspaper, had fallen partly through the floor. Great shafts of flame shot out of the bursting windows.

The printers stood in the street, broken glass at their feet. They embraced one another as the fire engines arrived. They were happy to be alive.

My father stood alone, struck numb by the last image of the burning presses.

The fire destroyed the printing presses. The plant had to close for repairs. But not one printer had been hurt.

Word Bank

fled *v.*: run away from
engulfed (en GULFD) *v.*: completely swallowed up
spewing (SPYOO ing) *v.*: throwing out with force
shafts *n.*: long columns
numb (NUM) *adj.*: without any feeling at all
image (IH muj) *n.*: picture in one's mind

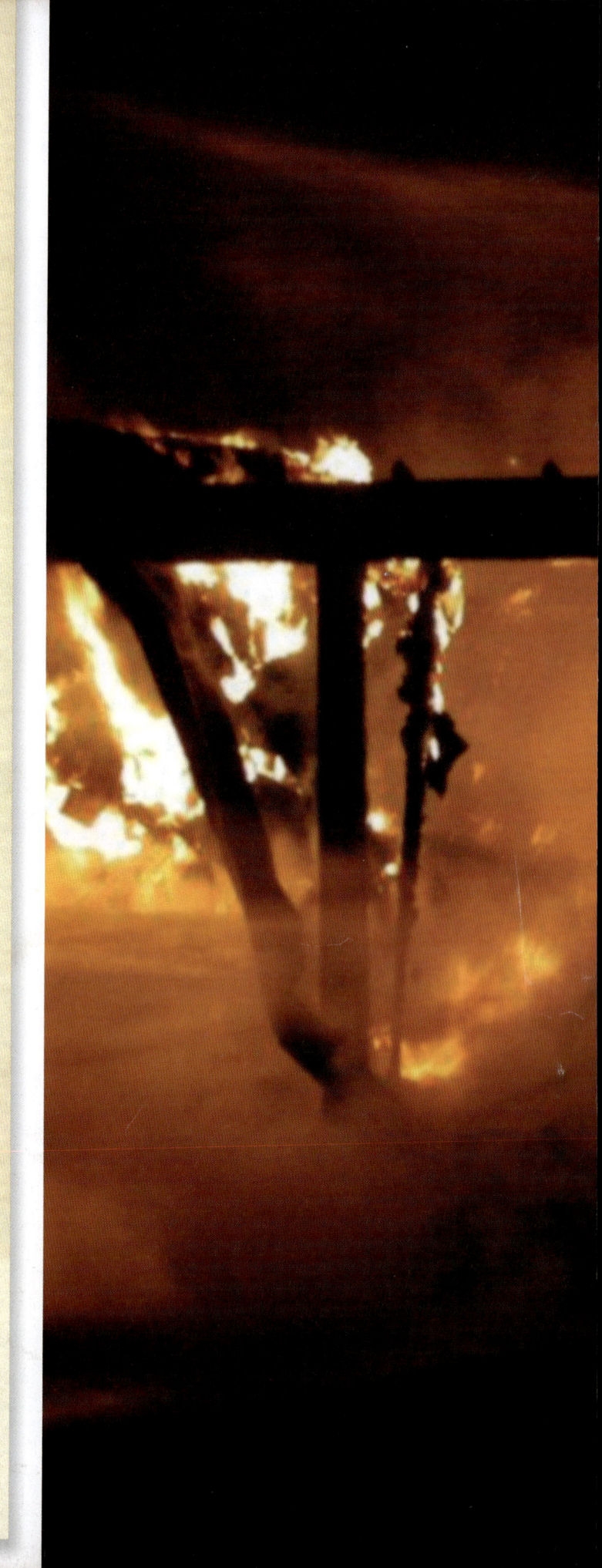

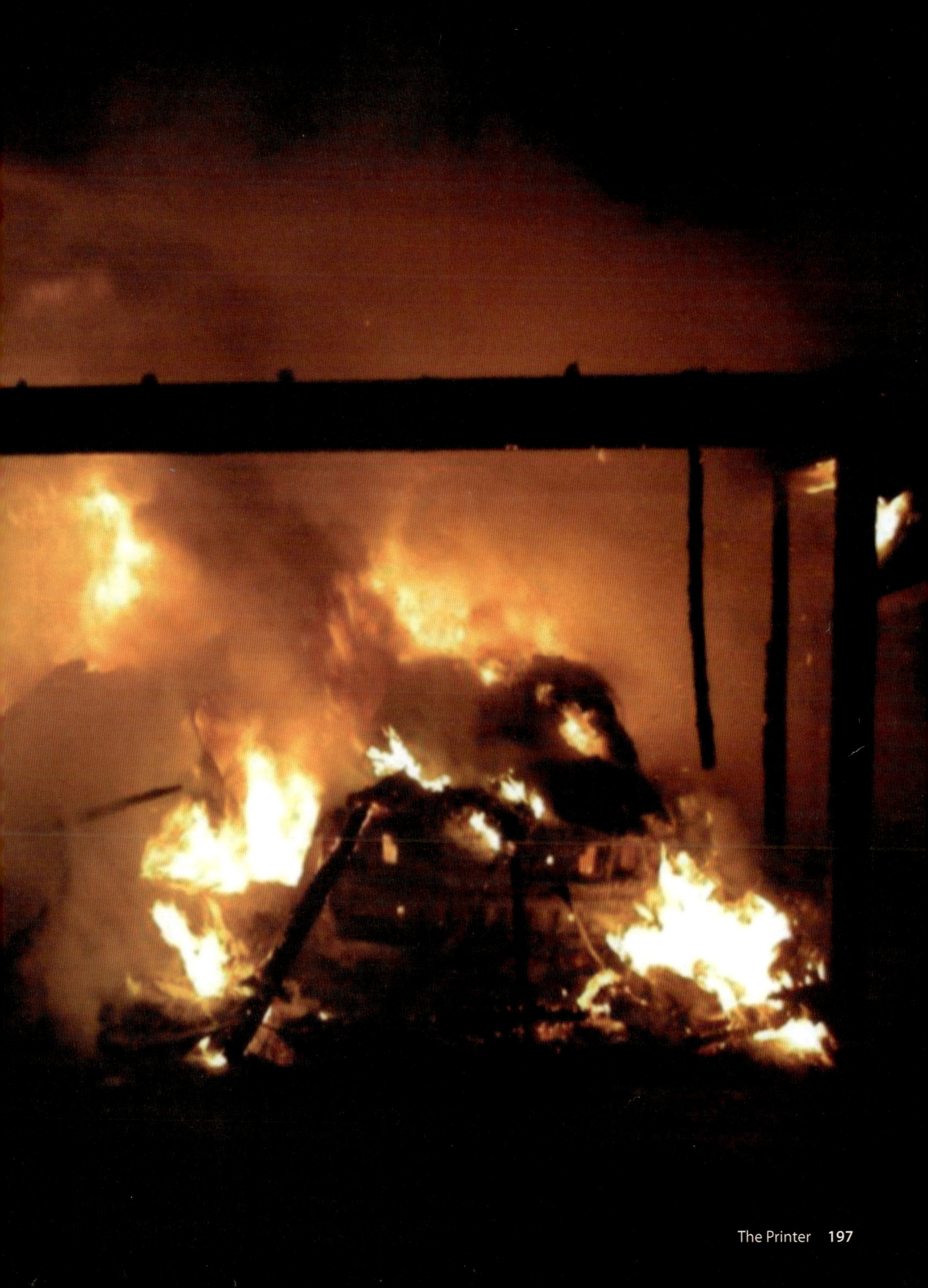

When the printing press finally reopened, my father went back to the work he loved. The new presses were switched on and roared into life.

When the day's newspaper had been printed, the presses shuddered to a stop. Now there was silence.

In the midst of the stillness, my father's co-workers gathered around him. They presented him with a hat made of the freshly printed newspaper.

And as my father put the hat on his head, all the printers who could hear did something surprising.

Word Bank

shuddered (SHUH derd) *v.*: shook slightly

midst *n.*: the middle of

They told him THANK YOU with their hands.

That night, my father picked up the newspaper hat that his fellow printers had given him. After adjusting the four corners, he placed it gently on my head. I didn't take off my hat, but wore it carefully to bed.

I imagined I was standing next to my father on a vast printing press floor, turning lead-type letters into words and sentences. We were wearing four-cornered newspaper hats.

We were printers.

About the Author

A hearing child of two deaf parents, **Myron Uhlberg**'s first language was American Sign Language. Myron learned spoken English by listening to the radio. From the age of six, he became his parents' ears and mouth. When Mr. Uhlberg was nine years old, he came with his parents to parent-teacher conferences to interpret between his parents and the teacher—and he was not always the easiest student! Mr. Uhlberg is a retired businessman who now writes children's books, some of which are based on his own experiences.

NEWSPAPER PRINTER'S HAT

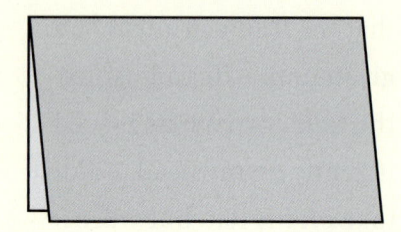

1. Take a full sheet of newspaper (4 printed pages with a fold in the center) and turn it sideways.

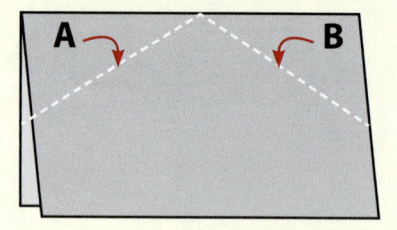

2. Fold down the corners A and B along the dotted lines.

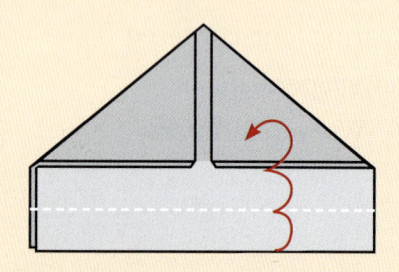

3. Fold up the top layer of the bottom edge twice.

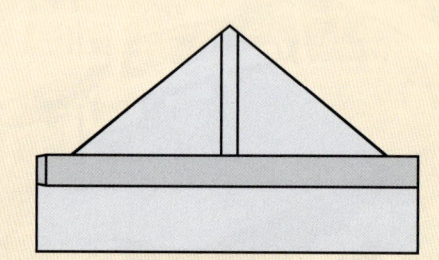

4. Turn the hat over.

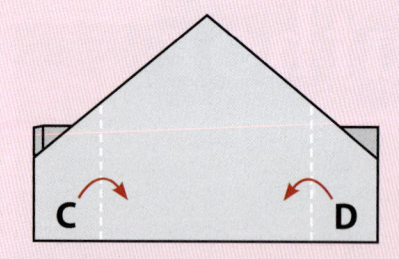

5. Fold the ends along the dotted lines C and D letting the edges of C and D meet in the center. (For larger heads, C and D are farther apart.)

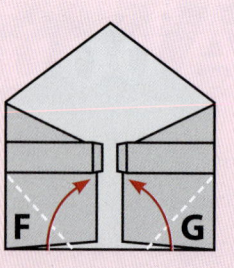

6. Fold corners F and G inward.

Why a newspaper hat?

With printing presses running at speeds up to 20 miles per hour and 70,000 newspapers being printed, trimmed, folded, and bound into bundles every hour, a fine mist of paper dust and ink is thrown into the air. Pressmen often fashion a paper hat like the one shown here to keep the ink and dust out of their hair.

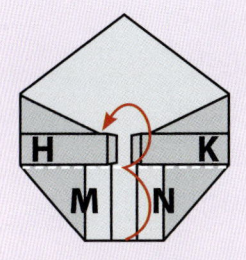

7. Fold the bottom flap up and over as shown, tucking MN in beneath HK.

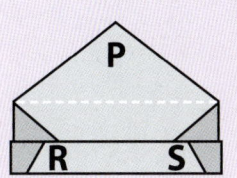

8. Fold the tip P down and tuck it beneath RS.

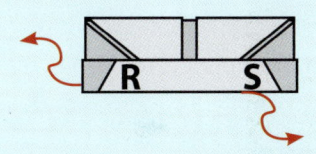

9. Insert thumbs into the bottom opening. Open and flatten out the hat to create a new square, where R and S meet.

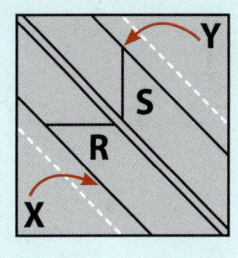

10. Fold in the tips X and Y and tuck them under R and S.

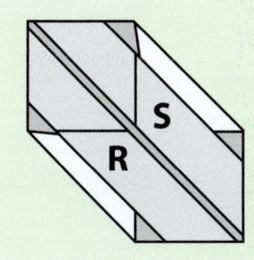

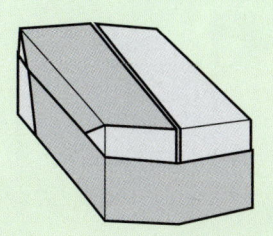

11. Then open out to form ----------→ Finished YOUR PRINTER'S HAT

The Printer   201

The Other Way to Listen

Byrd Baylor

I used to know
an old man
who could
walk
by any
cornfield
and hear
the corn
singing.

"Teach me,"
I'd say
when we'd
passed on by.
(I never said
a word
while he was
listening.)

"Just tell me
how
you learned
to hear
that
corn."

And he'd say,
"It takes
a lot of
practice.
You can't
be
in a hurry."

And I'd say,
"I have
the time."

He was so
 good
  at listening—
   once
    he heard
     wildflower seeds
      burst open,
       beginning
        to grow
         underground.

That's hard to do.

He said
 he was just
  lucky
   to have been
    by himself
     up there
      in the canyon
       after a rain.

He said
    it was the
        quietest place
            he'd ever been
            and he stayed there
            long enough to
            understand
            the quiet.

    I said,
        "I bet you were
        surprised
        when you heard
        those seeds."

But
he said,
"No,
I wasn't surprised at all.
It seemed like the most
    natural
        thing
            in the world."

        He just smiled,
            remembering.

Studying the Selection

FIRST IMPRESSIONS
If you were working alongside someone who was deaf, would you ignore him?

QUICK REVIEW

1. What did the father do each evening after reading the day's paper?
2. How did the father speak to others?
3. What was the first thing the father did to alert the other printers to the danger?
4. After the fire, what did the printers do to thank the father for warning them about the fire?

FOCUS

5. At the beginning of the story, the father put a four-cornered newspaper hat on his son's head. At the end of the story, the printers put one on the father's head. What is the meaning of putting a newspaper hat on someone's head?
6. We learn something about the father's personality from the story. Write down three personality traits that the father had. Next to each one, write down how you know that about the father. For example, the father is a hard worker. We know this because he has worked hard at his job for many years.

CREATING AND WRITING

7. Your assignment is to produce the front page of the newspaper on the day following the fire. Your teacher will divide your class into groups. Each group will write one article for the front page of the paper. One article will describe the fire. One will describe how the father and the other deaf printers alerted everyone else. One article will be about the newspaper company's plans for rebuilding the plant after the fire. The last group will write an article about fire prevention. In each group, one student may draw a "photograph" to illustrate the article.
8. Your teacher will provide your class with newspaper and you will make a four-cornered newspaper hat. Put it on and wear it for a while!

The Printer 205

Jill's Journal:
On Assignment Visiting the Wheelers in New Jersey

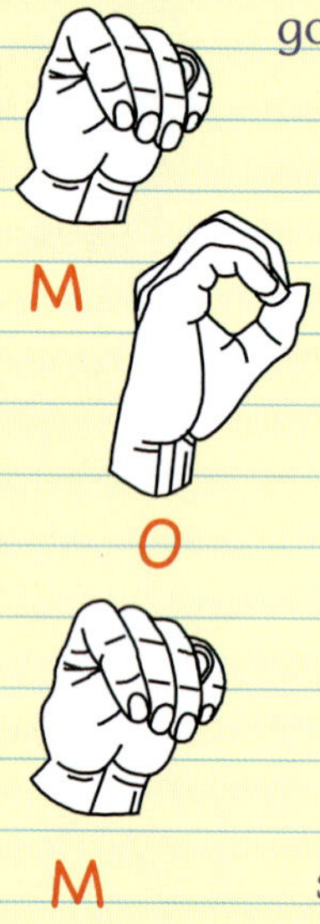

A good friend told me about the Wheeler family and I wanted to meet them. Dr. and Mrs. Wheeler and their two children live in a white shingled house on a quiet street. Every day, Dr. Wheeler goes off to his job as a veterinarian. He is an animal doctor. Mrs. Wheeler works part-time at the courthouse. She is an attorney for people who are deaf. In fact, both Dr. and Mrs. Wheeler are deaf. Dr. Wheeler works with several other animal doctors who are deaf. Mrs. Wheeler works with an interpreter. Both Dr. and Mrs. Wheeler use a special language that they make with their hands. It is called American Sign Language, or ASL. American Sign Language does not come from English, but is commonly used in the United States.

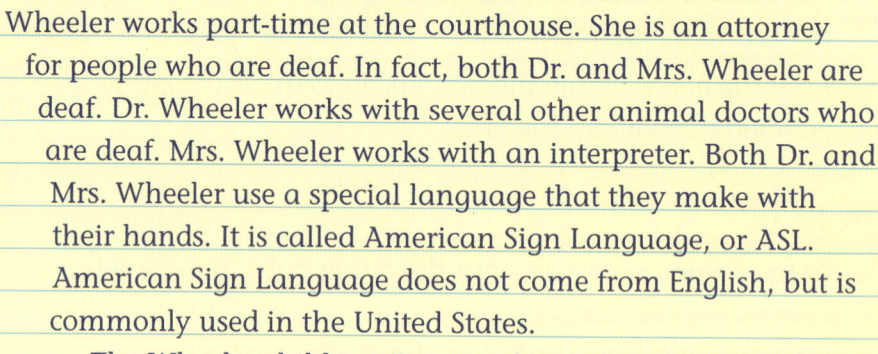

The Wheeler children, Betsy and Wendy, can hear. Both girls go to regular public schools and have many friends. Betsy is especially good in English and art, and Wendy's best school subject is math, and she enjoys sports. They both read a lot.

Betsy and Wendy are just like regular kids. But children who can hear, whose parents are deaf, learn two separate languages when they are toddlers. One language they can hear with their ears and speak with their mouths. The other they make with signs that they form with their fingers.

I have been told that hearing children whose parents are deaf often feel like they live in two different worlds: the world of deaf people and the hearing world of their teachers, friends, and other relatives. Most hearing people have not been around deaf people and their families.

It may surprise you to learn that there are more than 28 million deaf and hard of hearing people in the United States. I didn't know that. I also didn't know that more than 90% of deaf parents have children who can hear. I wanted to learn more about families with deaf parents and hearing children so I went to visit the Wheelers.

I have brought along an expert interpreter, Jane Wills, so that she can translate Dr. and Mrs. Wheeler's sign language for me. I did not want to use Betsy and Wendy as interpreters—even though they know ASL and English.

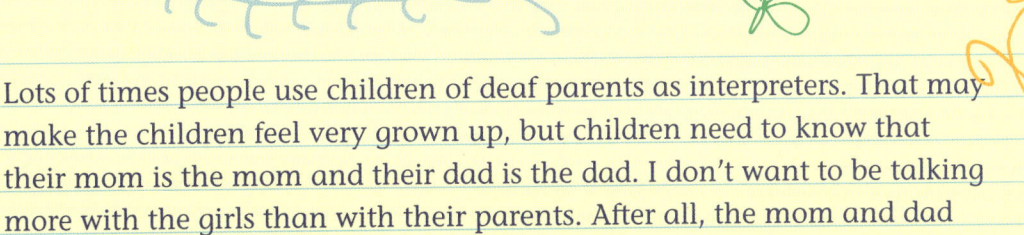

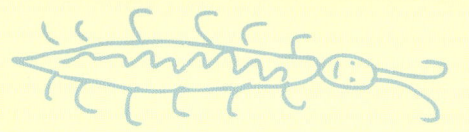

Lots of times people use children of deaf parents as interpreters. That may make the children feel very grown up, but children need to know that their mom is the mom and their dad is the dad. I don't want to be talking more with the girls than with their parents. After all, the mom and dad are the ones who make the rules and the decisions in this family.

I knock on their front door and I am greeted first by a barking golden retriever. Mrs. Wheeler opens the door and signs that one of the advantages of being deaf is that you can't hear the dog's barking!

Betsy and Wendy introduce themselves. When I follow Mrs. Wheeler into the kitchen, I see that Dr. Wheeler is on the phone—a special TTY phone that changes sound to printed words. He waves hello.

Betsy says, "It's an emergency call from the animal hospital. When he took the call, Dad said to tell you that he would try to make it short."

Mrs. Wheeler, Jane Wills, and the girls and I sit down at the large oak table. Mrs. Wheeler signs that the kitchen is the best place to meet, because then she can keep an eye on the food that is cooking on the stove. The doorbell rings and a light flashes on and off above the kitchen door.

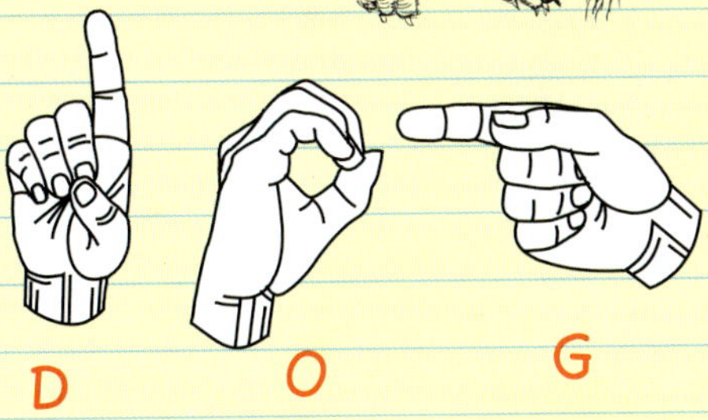

The dog barks and Wendy says, "It must be the newspaper boy. He wants to get paid."

She jumps up, takes several dollars from a jar on the counter, and leaves the room.

Mrs. Wheeler signs, "With the dog—even though we can't hear him—we hardly need the flashing light!" Then she speaks more seriously through Jane. "It is hard for us—deaf people—to feel like we are part of the hearing world. People don't learn to sign, so we can't speak to just anyone. Even though my husband and I have good jobs, we cannot feel like hearing people."

Dr. Wheeler has finished his call and takes a chair at the table. Jane and I are introduced to him. He signs, "I remember when the girls were babies, and I worried how we would hear their cries. Sometimes we slept with a hand in the baby's crib to feel the vibrations when they awoke. You know, every sound makes a vibration that you can feel with your hands or feet. Now there are lots of devices that change sound to light."

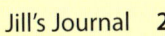

Jill's Journal

CAN YOU HEAR ME NOW

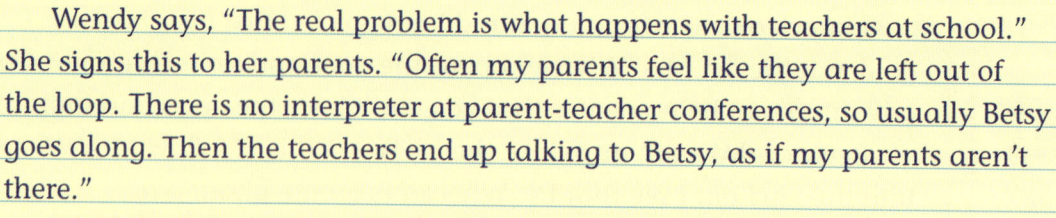

Wendy says, "The real problem is what happens with teachers at school." She signs this to her parents. "Often my parents feel like they are left out of the loop. There is no interpreter at parent-teacher conferences, so usually Betsy goes along. Then the teachers end up talking to Betsy, as if my parents aren't there."

I find that I have to keep reminding myself to pay attention to Dr. and Mrs. Wheeler. It is as if I want to take the easy way out and just speak to the girls. Then I don't have to wait for my words to be signed, and wait again for an answer from Jane. Is this the way that most hearing people react? Why does it

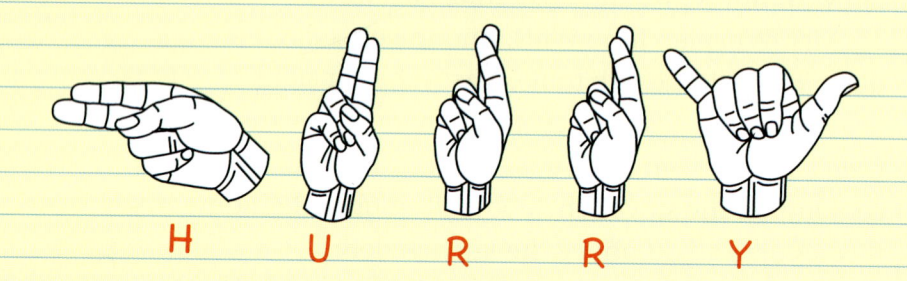

H U R R Y

feel difficult to wait? I am in no hurry. After all, this is why I came here!

Betsy says, "Sometimes people shout loudly at my parents, as if they think they could hear them if they shout." Then, she signs her words.

"How does that make you feel?" I ask her.

"It makes me feel embarrassed. Then I try to understand why people might shout."

We continue talking until it is dark out. The signing and waiting has become easier for me. I am glad for this.

Mrs. Wheeler says, "Deaf parents should have honest discussions with their hearing children about what to do when people treat deaf people badly. We try to give them 'what to do' suggestions when those situations arise. Then, hopefully, they are less upset and less embarrassed."

I say that I have heard that deaf parents are caring and have excellent relationships with their hearing children. Then I add, "I know that it is late and we all have to be up early tomorrow for work and school. I am very grateful for your having me into your wonderful home and talking with me."

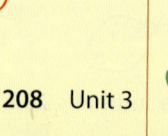

W A I T

I leave the Wheelers knowing so much more about the lives of deaf parents with hearing children. What a fine family they are. I hope I have a chance to spend time with them again. I think I am going to work on learning ASL!

POWER SKILL:
Finger Spelling

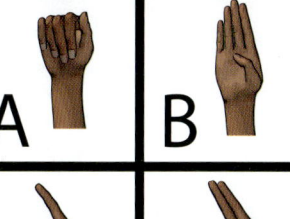

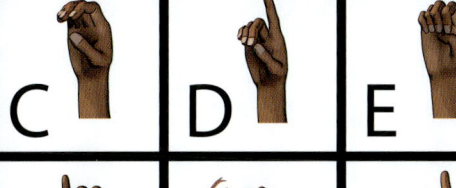

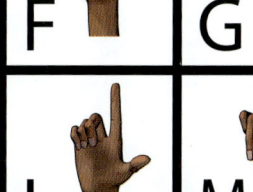

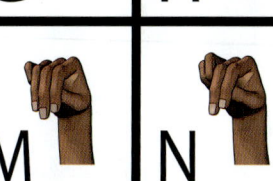

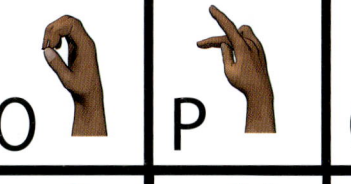

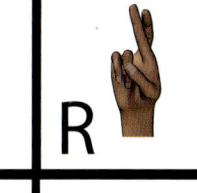

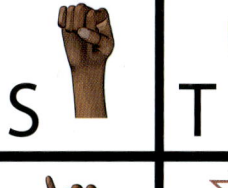

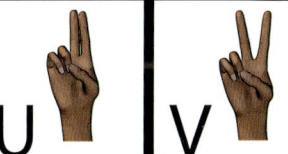

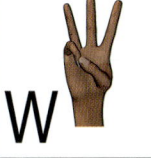

American Sign Language Finger Spelling

A B C D E F G H I J K L M N O P Q R S T U V W X Y Z

1. Using the American Sign Language finger spelling chart, teach yourself how to finger spell your name.

2. Teach yourself to finger spell the following:
   How are you?
   I am fine.
   What is your name?

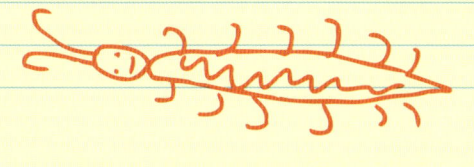

Jill's Journal

Lesson in Literature...
JoJo and Midnight

WHAT IS POINT OF VIEW?

- **Point of view** means the way *you* see things.
- The same events can be reported differently if two different people are reporting them from two different points of view.
- A story is usually told from the narrator's point of view. If there are two narrators, there will be two points of view.
- As people mature, they try to see things from another person's point of view as well as from their own.

THINK ABOUT IT!

1. What are the two points of view in the story?
2. Does JoJo understand Midnight's point of view about eating? Bring proof of your answer.
3. JoJo and Midnight report on a single event in two completely different ways. Write two sentences. In the first, describe Midnight's leap through the air from JoJo's point of view. In the second, describe Midnight's leap through the air from Midnight's point of view.

JoJo's Story

It's a sunny, hot day today, just like I like it. Only Midnight, my wonderful black cat, does not like it hot. I want him to like what I like, so we can enjoy it together. What's worse is that he doesn't like water. Oh, he likes it to drink, but not to fool around in. I hope he is not going to spoil our fun this morning.

Midnight's Story

Well, meow. That is what I have to say. I love my JoJo. But he should know by now that I tire easily. After I have my delicious breakfast of Meaty Bittles, it is time for a nap. See JoJo, see how I am yawning and stretching my front legs out. It's the perfect position for rolling on my back in the dust and taking a rest.

JoJo's Story

Oh, that cat! I see right now he is giving me a big yawn and stretching a lot, to show how tired he is. After he eats he has to lick his paws and wash around his mouth. (Actually, I like how clean and shiny he is.) Let me tell you, every time he eats it's a great big deal. Then, of course, he has to rest. Sometimes he stands in the open doorway and takes a few minutes to decide whether he is going to go in or out. I find that irritating, but I am told it's a cat thing.

Midnight's Story

Yes, I'm a cat. You know I'm smarter than a dog, and dogs are pretty smart. I don't miss much. I can see that new pool the Señor and Señora bought for JoJo. I know he is excited to go swimming in there. He is going to want company, and cats hate water! He's going to say his friends are out of town. Now what does that mean—out of town? Do I ever get to go out of town? I wouldn't know if I were out of town, because I wouldn't know where I was! I yawn again, S-L-O-W-L-Y, so he can admire my wonderful cat fangs, and it's time for a rest under the lawn chair.

Lorenzo & Angelina

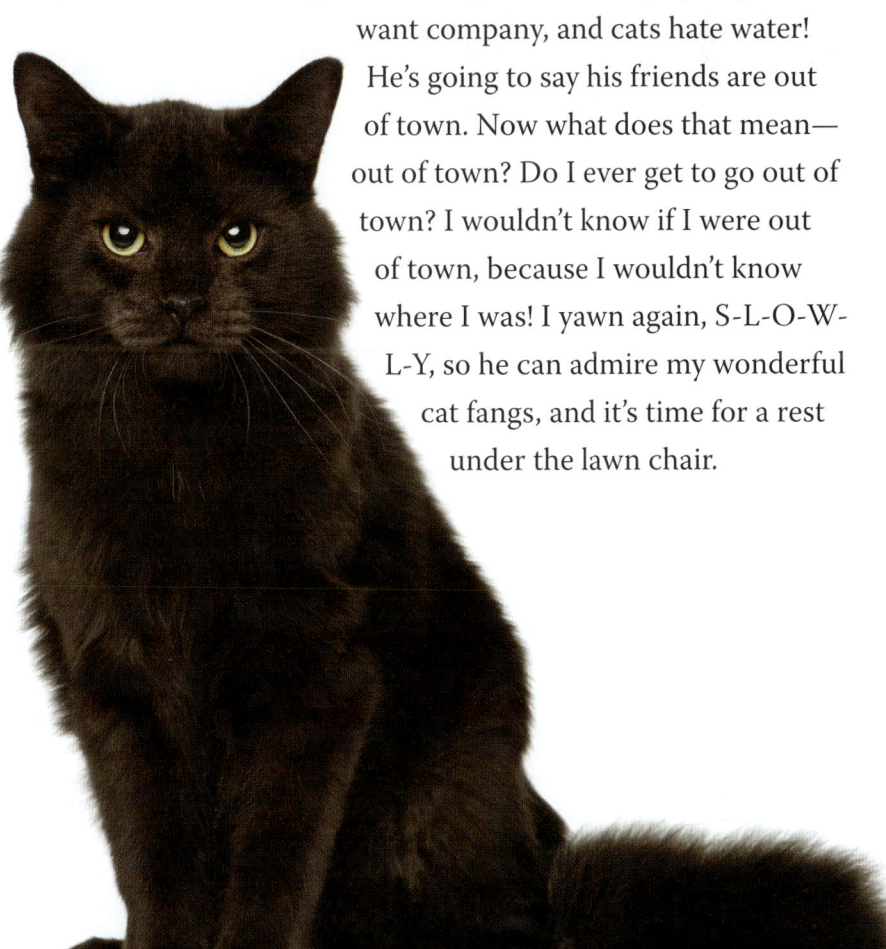

Blueprint for Reading

INTO . . . *Lorenzo & Angelina*

Have you ever wondered what an animal was thinking? Do you go to the zoo and feel like the monkeys are making fun of you? Do you talk to your dog and imagine that he's talking back to you? Well, here is your chance to read a story that tells you just what an animal is thinking. Angelina is a girl who owns a donkey named Lorenzo. Although donkeys cannot talk, in this story we are told what Lorenzo is thinking. As you read the story, ask yourself: Who is wiser, the girl or the donkey?

EYES ON *Point of View*

Sunny skies! Fluffy clouds! Warm weather! Fantastic—right? Not if you own a ski lodge and you need snow for your business. Thunder! Lightning! Rain! Miserable—right? Not if you're a farmer waiting for your fields to be watered. It all depends on your **point of view**, your individual way of seeing things. Lorenzo and Angelina have two different points of view and there is a constant struggle between them. Angelina expresses her opinion by shouting at Lorenzo and stamping her foot. Lorenzo, being a donkey, can only express his opinion by refusing to budge. It seems they will never agree! Until one day, something happens to change all that. As you read *Lorenzo & Angelina*, ask yourself what *your* point of view would be if you were there.

Lorenzo & Angelina

Eugene Fern

Angelina's[1] Story

Every morning, when the air is fresh and the dew lies like shining jewels over the fields and trees, I go to Lorenzo's[2] stable. I carry with me the milk which Umberto[3] has put into a heavy wooden barrel and the eggs which Jacinta has carefully packed in a wooden box. I open the door and out comes Lorenzo. "Good morning, my Lorenzo," I say. I pat his back, rub the top of his head, and give him a hug. Then I pack the barrel and box on him and I am ready to leave for the village.

But not Lorenzo!

---
1. *Angelina* (AHN heh lee nuh)
2. *Lorenzo* (lohr REN zo)
3. *Umberto* (um BAIR toh)

Lorenzo's Story

Every morning, when Angelina comes to let me out of my house, she is glad to see me. She rubs my head, puts her face next to mine, gives me a squeeze, and says, "Good morning, my Lorenzo."

And every morning, to be sure, I am glad to see her too—that is, until she starts to scold.

Lorenzo & Angelina

Angelina's Story

Every morning it is the same. I talk to him politely, but he looks this way and that. He smells the air. He chews the grass. He nibbles at the clover. He does everything but what he is supposed to do!

I begin to lose my temper, of course. I shout at him. He pays no attention. He stands like a rock.

Though I love him dearly, there is no doubt that my Lorenzo is the most stubborn creature in the whole world.

Lorenzo's Story

Every morning, Angelina says, "Lorenzo, it is time for us to go to the village, so please begin to walk." But anyone should know I am not yet ready to go. I have to smell the morning air. I have to chew the grass under the eucalyptus tree.

"Lorenzo," she says, "let us go this very minute." But I am still too busy. "Move, you stubborn donkey!" she screams. "Move those stubborn feet!"

But of course I have to see if the house is in the right place, if the south fence has moved, if the sheep are where they're supposed to be. Naturally, I cannot leave yet.

It is only when she stamps her feet that I move. I am very fond of Angelina and don't like to see her upset, but is it not wrong for her to insult me this way?

Angelina's Story

One morning, like all the other times, we finally set out for the village. My stubborn Lorenzo had finished whatever it was he was doing, and I could tell by the way his ears stood straight up and by the quick movements of his feet that he was as pleased as I to leave for the marketplace at Cuzoroca.[4]

---

4. *Cuzoroca* (KOO zoh ROH kah)

Lorenzo's Story

One morning we finally set out for the village. Angelina had finished shouting and stamping. As always, she was happy once we started. I could tell by the way she began to sing and laugh—and every once in a while to skip along the road. She liked the little trip to the village, and, to tell the truth, so did I.

Angelina's Story

However, this day was to be different, for I had decided to go to the top of El Padre[5] Mountain! Ever since I can remember, I had heard of the beauty and the glory to be seen from there. It is said that from the top of El Padre one can touch the sky.

   I was so excited about my great adventure that I hardly knew where I was going.

Lorenzo's Story

This day was like all other days. We went beside El Padre Mountain, through Quesada[6] Pass, across the flat meadows, through the forest, and into the village.

---

5. *El Padre* (el PAHD ree)
6. *Quesada* (kay SAH dah)

Lorenzo & Angelina

Angelina's Story

When we came to the marketplace, I quickly took care of my business with Señor Vives. He counted the eggs, weighed the milk, and paid me for them. I thanked him politely and then I climbed on Lorenzo's back. I could hardly wait to begin the trip to the top of El Padre Mountain!

As one might expect, when we came to the crossroads my stubborn donkey refused to move. Only after much shouting did he agree to take the right fork instead of the left.

Lorenzo's Story

Señor Vives was at his place, as usual. He took the milk and eggs from my back, counted the eggs, weighed the milk, and paid Angelina for them. As usual, he took the money from his strong little box under the counter. Then, as usual, we started for home.

But things no longer went as usual, for Angelina decided to go home a different way. Instead of taking the left turn after the road leaves the forest, she decided to take the right. At first I wouldn't budge. Who knows what might be in a strange land? Finally, with all her shouting, I gave in and went where *she* wanted to go!

Angelina's Story

This road was different from the hard dirt road leading to our farm. It passed over rushing streams, between tall trees and huge rocks, always moving up—higher and higher. It was rough and rocky, and the higher we went, the rougher it got. Though I knew the sun would soon be sinking, I was determined to reach the top of El Padre Mountain. Lorenzo moved more and more slowly, but I urged him on.

Soon the road had almost disappeared. There was nothing ahead of us but a little rocky path. It was getting dark and Lorenzo stopped. Again I had to shout and scold until he moved on.

Lorenzo's Story

This road was not like the other. It was rough and rocky. It did not go through Quesada Pass but behind it, toward the top of El Padre Mountain. Higher and higher we climbed, and the higher we went, the harder it was to see the road. Soon there was no road at all, just a rocky path.

And still Angelina had to explore!

Once or twice I stopped, but she shouted so much that I kept moving. It was growing dark, and we were up so high I could hardly breathe. There were rocks on all sides, and every once in a while a poor little bush.

Angelina's Story

Though the wind was stronger and the path even rockier than before, I was not worried. My Lorenzo is as sure-footed as a mountain goat and I knew he would not fall. Besides, any moment I expected to see the glory and beauty of our country, and this would make everything worthwhile.

But once more my stubborn donkey refused to go. Again I had to scream to make him move those stubborn legs.

Lorenzo's Story

I was getting worried. It was not easy to walk, and I knew that if I stumbled we would have a long fall before we reached the good earth again.

So once more I stopped, but my little Angelina insisted on climbing that mountain. She shouted. "Stubborn, stubborn donkey!" she screamed at me.

So what was there to do but move higher and still higher?

Lorenzo & Angelina

Angelina's Story

It was when we came to two huge rocks that stood like sentinels[7] over the others that Lorenzo made up his mind not to move another inch. He sat down in front of the rocks in such a way that not even a tiny lizard could pass by.

Lorenzo's Story

Finally, what seemed to be the path went between two huge rocks. And then it ended! A bush grew between the rocks, and after that—who knows?

This time I decided the trip was over. Not another step would I take! I sat down.

Angelina's Story

I yelled at Lorenzo. I shouted. I pleaded. I screamed. I pulled at him. I pushed him from behind. He would not budge. He sat there looking like one more rock, among all the others.

Lorenzo's Story

The great explorer Angelina did not take to this kindly. Her shouts before were as nothing compared to the noise she now made. "Move!" she screamed. "We are almost at the top!" She pushed and pulled me. Tears of anger were in her eyes, but it did no good. This time I would not take another step.

---

7. A *sentinel* is a person who stands watch, like a guard. The two huge rocks *stood like sentinels*, guarding the path.

Lorenzo & Angelina   225

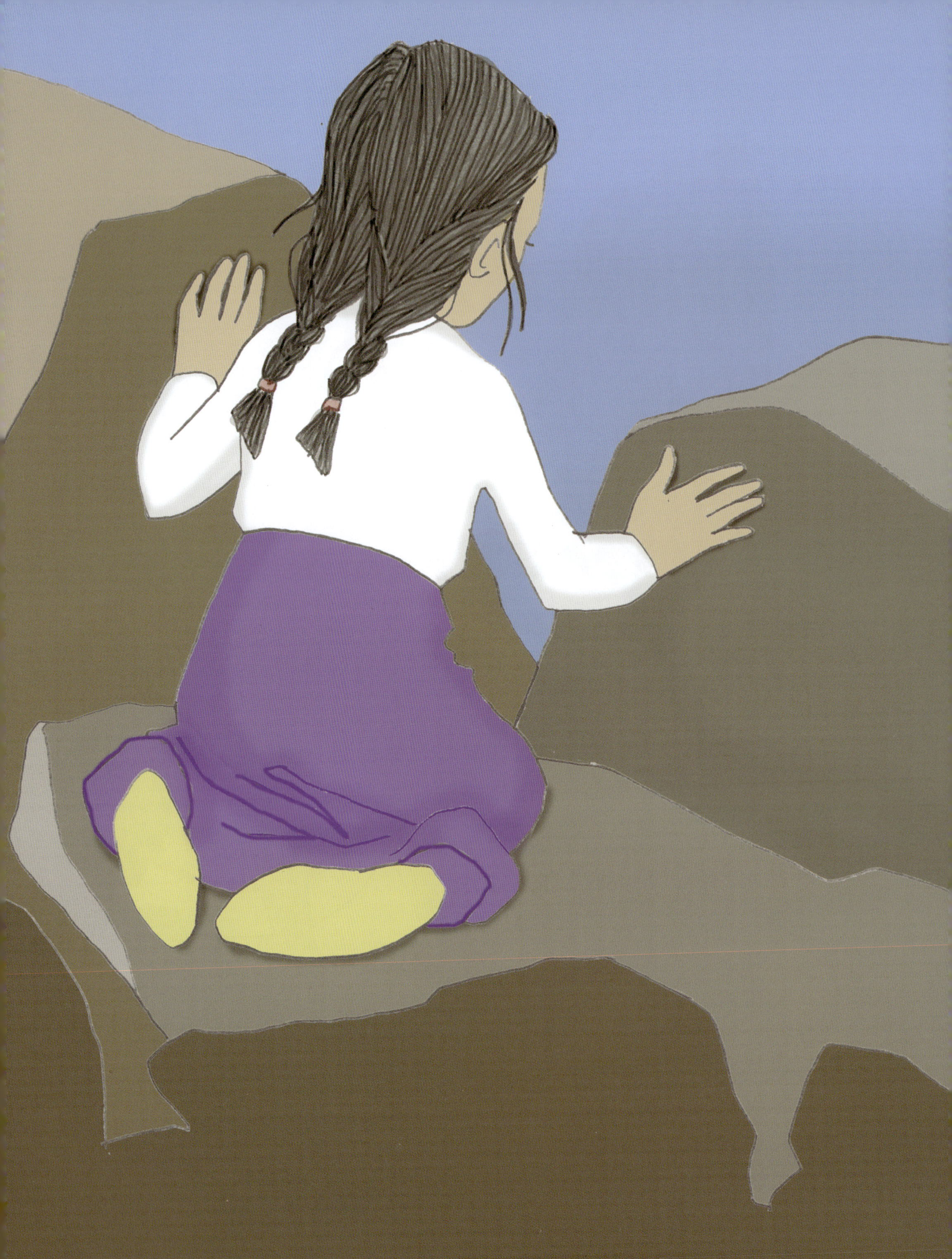

Angelina's Story

At this very moment I heard footsteps, and there behind us appeared my father, followed by Señor Vives and Señor Quiñones[8] of the police. Suddenly I realized how late it must be. I was sure Papá would be furious. Instead he picked me up and kissed me. All he said was:

"Little one, I am not angry because you took the right turn instead of the left. Children are always looking for new paths. This I understand. But why have you stayed so long? Didn't you know your mother and I would be worried? Everyone is looking for you."

I tried to explain how much I wanted to see the glory of the world from the top of El Padre Mountain and how much time I had wasted trying to get that stubborn Lorenzo to move.

Lorenzo's Story

Suddenly there were sounds behind us and who should appear but Señor Garcia, Señor Vives, and Señor Quiñones of the police! How happy they were to see us! Señor Garcia picked up little Angelina. He hugged her and whispered to her, while the other gentlemen, with big smiles, slapped him on the back.

Angelina looked ashamed and said, "I did so much want to see the top of the mountain, Papá, but that stubborn Lorenzo would not move. He simply refused to budge."

---

8. *Quiñones* (KEE nohn nais)

Angelina's Story

Papá said nothing. He took my hand and led me between the two huge rocks. He pushed the little bush aside so I could see beyond it. I looked and my knees turned to water! Beyond the bush was the end of the path and also the end of the mountain. Had Lorenzo and I taken but one step beyond the bush, we should never have taken a step again!

Lorenzo's Story

Señor Garcia did not say a word. He took Angelina by the hand and led her between the two rocks. Beyond the bush was nothing—no path, no rocks, just nothing.

It was, of course, as *I* suspected. What could one expect to find up here so near the sky, where even the poorest bush finds it difficult to breathe?

Angelina said nothing. She just stood there, pale and trembling. My poor Angelina!

Angelina's Story

I do not remember too clearly what happened after that, for I was weak from fear and could hardly stand. But I do remember one thing. Seeing that dear, stubborn donkey standing there, I felt such a love for him that I kissed him gently and whispered, "Thank you, my Lorenzo!"

Lorenzo & Angelina

Lorenzo's Story

Señor Garcia said, "You should be grateful to have such a stubborn donkey, my little flower. If not for him, I would have neither Angelina nor Lorenzo." He put his arms around my neck and gave me such a squeeze that I could hardly breathe. When Angelina kissed me, my happiness was complete.

About the Author

Though **Eugene Fern** wrote children's books, he was primarily an artist. He illustrated his own books, and he worked for many years as a professor of art, artist, and illustrator. He also enlisted in the U.S. Air Force, in which he served in Alaska and became a sergeant. Mr. Fern enjoys anything artistic and creative, including music, dance, literature, and architecture.

Studying the Selection

FIRST IMPRESSIONS
Have you ever been *so* sure about something and then found out you were *so* wrong?

QUICK REVIEW

1. Who are Lorenzo and Angelina?
2. What was Angelina's dream?
3. When they reached the two rocks, why did Lorenzo refuse to go a step further?
4. How did Angelina feel about Lorenzo when she was shown how dangerous the mountain was?

FOCUS

5. If Lorenzo could have spoken, do you think he could have convinced Angelina not to climb the mountain? Why or why not?
6. Can you explain what is different and unusual about the way this story is written?

CREATING AND WRITING

7. Whenever policemen return from a call, they write out a report of what happened. Imagine that Señor Vives and Señor Quiñones of the police wrote a report about Angelina and Lorenzo and all that had happened. Write their report and include in it their opinion of Angelina and Lorenzo.
8. For this activity you will play a game that will show you how the same event can cause completely different reactions in different people. That is because we do not have the same point of view. Your teacher will tell you the rules and help you play "Who Am I?" Enjoy!

Lorenzo & Angelina 231

Lesson in Literature...

When Snow Days Come, Dogs Have Beards

RELATIONSHIPS IN A STORY

- A **relationship** is the way two characters in a story connect with one another.
- A relationship may involve strong feelings such as love or hate.
- A relationship may remain the same throughout the story.
- Relationships between characters may change from the beginning to the end of the story.

THINK ABOUT IT!

1. What evidence can you find in the story that Mom is very considerate of Dad?
2. How do Will and Sarah relate to the dog with the beard?
3. What do you think is the relationship between the children and their father?

It is winter and we are watching an explosion of snow. My sister keeps saying, "Oh, how beautiful." And she is right. It is really beautiful. It looks like the sky is wearing a gown that grows closer and closer to the ground. But it bothers me when she says it many times. I guess I am not a patient person.

Hey, though, it's a snow day! Hurray! No school. Just fun. Maybe we'll go sledding! But I look outside and I see a dog shivering in the bushes with icicles for a little beard. Am I really seeing what I think I am seeing? My father has a lot of strange expressions, and one of them is: *When snow days come, dogs have beards.*

When he uses one of his strange expressions, we look at him and wait for some of the others. We suspect that my mom thinks these sayings are silly, but she never says anything to dampen Dad's enthusiasm. My father is a joyful person.

We are all in the kitchen and we're making pancakes. So who's here? I'm Rosalie, the oldest (I'm twelve years old). My brother, Steve, is next at ten. Ella, who thinks the snow is so beautiful, is eight. Then comes a couple of younger ones, Will and Sarah, who have to do as they're told—and get very mad when I tease them with that.

My dad is here to help us make complicated snow forts after we're done making pancakes. (Also, he could not get the car out of the driveway.) He is looking out the picture window onto the backyard and scratching his head. He says to my mom, "You aren't going to believe this, but in addition to the squirrels and the birds and the deer who are eating the bread and seed you put out there, there is really a *dog with a beard*! And he doesn't look very happy."

"Yes, yes," I say quietly. "He looks so lonely."

Will and Sarah shout, "He must be very cold and shivery."

Ella runs to the window and cries, "Mom! We've got to do something for that dog. He looks like he's wearing a snow suit."

"Yes," says Steve. "You both taught us to care for all living things. And as Dad says, *Mice are twice as nice, but dogs are better than frogs.*"

Dad throws open the back door and tiptoes outside. "Come come, little dog," he utters softly.

The dog, one of those short dogs that already have a mustache, hops through the snow and leaps into Dad's outstretched arms.

Mom says, "Now don't everyone crowd around and scare the little guy."

We each approach the pooch as he curls up in my dad's arms. We pet it gently. Mom says, "Give it space so it can breathe!" We dry the dog with a thick towel. Dad asks, "Does he still have a beard, or did it melt?"

I put a little cooked hamburger down on a saucer. Dad sets the dog on the floor and it gobbles all of the food. Then Will brings over a bowl of water. Sarah pets the dog's head as it laps water. This really is a wonderful family event.

The dog has no collar or tags. Maybe we can keep it. Ella says the dog is much more pleasing than mice or frogs.

Blueprint for Reading

INTO . . . *A Day When Frogs Wear Shoes*

It's a hot summer day and there's nothing to do. Have you ever had a day like that? If you have, then you know that the boredom is even worse than the heat. The kids think about going on a hike, but Dad says that the ground is so hot, even the frogs are wearing shoes. What should they do? In the days before people had air conditioned homes, the best way to escape the heat was to go down to the nearest ocean, lake, river, or creek, and jump in! In *A Day When Frogs Wear Shoes*, Dad takes the kids to the river to cool off. While he rests, they search for frogs wearing shoes. Do you think they'll find any?

EYES ON *Connections and Relationships*

Who are you? You are your mother's child, your friend's friend, your teacher's student—you are many things to many people. How you behave often depends on how you feel when you are near a particular person. You may be quiet near your teacher but loud near your friend. You may be respectful to your father but bossy to your little sister. One way we learn about characters in a story is by seeing how they connect with each other. As we read the story, we think about what the characters *say* to one another, what they *do* to one another, and how they *think* about one another. Some people consider the connections, or relationships, between characters to be the most interesting part of any story. As you read A *Day When Frogs Wear Shoes*, you will find that the father and children have a very special relationship. Can you describe it?

A Day When Frogs Wear Shoes

from *More Stories Julian Tells* by Ann Cameron

My little brother, Huey, my best friend, Gloria, and I were sitting on our front steps. It was one of those hot summer days when everything stands still. We didn't know what to do. We were watching the grass grow. It didn't grow fast.

"You know something?" Gloria said. "This is a slow day."

"It's so slow the dogs don't bark," Huey said.

"It's so slow the flies don't fly," Gloria said.

"It's so slow the ice cream wouldn't melt," I said.

"If we had any ice cream," Huey said.

"But we don't," Gloria said.

We watched the grass some more.

"We better do something," I said.

"Like what?" Gloria asked.

"We could go visit Dad," Huey said.

"That's a terrible idea," I said.

"Why?" Huey asked. "I like visiting Dad."

My father has a shop about a mile from our house, where he fixes cars. Usually it is fun to visit him. If he has customers, he always introduces us as if we were important guests. If he doesn't have company, sometimes he lets us ride in the cars he puts up on the lift. Sometimes he buys us treats.

"Huey," I said, "usually, visiting Dad is a good idea. Today, it's a dangerous idea."

"Why?" Gloria said.

"Because we're bored," I said. "My dad hates it when people are bored. He says the world is so interesting nobody should ever be bored."

"I see," Gloria said, as if she didn't.

"So we'll go see him," Huey said, "and we just won't tell him we're bored. We're bored, but we won't tell him."

"Just so you remember that!" I said.

"Oh, I'll remember," Huey said.

Huey was wearing his angel look. When he has that look, you know he'll never remember anything.

Huey and I put on sweat bands. Gloria put on dark glasses. We started out.

The sun shined up at us from the sidewalks. Even the shadows on the street were hot as blankets.

Huey picked up a stick and scratched it along the sidewalk. "Oh, we're bored," he muttered. "Bored, bored, bored, bored, bored!"

236 Unit 3

A Day When Frogs Wear Shoes   237

"Huey!" I yelled. I wasn't bored anymore. I was nervous. Finally we reached a sign:

> **RALPH'S CAR HOSPITAL**
> Punctures
> Rust
> Dents & Bashes
> Bad Brakes
> Bad Breaks
> Unusual Complaints

That's my dad's sign. My dad is Ralph.

The parking lot had three cars in it. Dad was inside the shop, lifting the hood of another car. He didn't have any customers with him, so we didn't get to shake hands and feel like visiting mayors or congressmen.

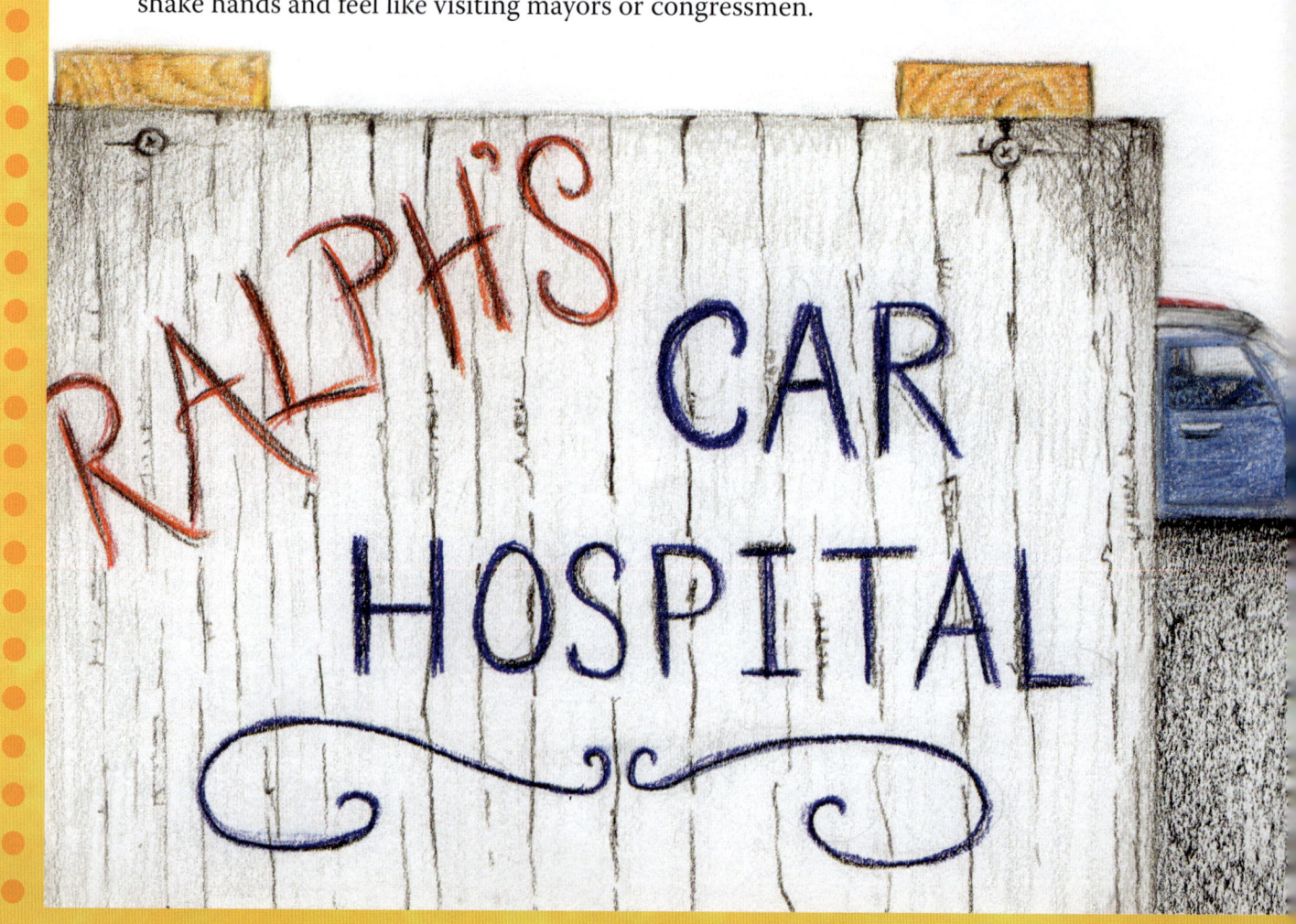

"Hi, Dad," I said.

"Hi!" my dad said.

"We're—" Huey said.

I didn't trust Huey. I stepped on his foot.

"We're on a hike," I said.

"Well, nice of you to stop by," my father said. "If you want, you can stay awhile and help me."

"O.K.," we said.

So Huey sorted nuts and bolts. Gloria shined fenders with a rag. I held a new windshield wiper while my dad put it on a car window.

"Nice work, Huey and Julian and Gloria!" my dad said when we were done.

And then he sent us to the store across the street to buy paper cups and ice cubes and a can of frozen lemonade.

We mixed the lemonade in the shop. Then we sat out under the one tree by the side of the driveway and drank all of it.

"Good lemonade!" my father said. "So what are you kids going to do now?"

"Oh, hike!" I said.

"You know," my father answered, "I'm surprised at you kids picking a hot day like today for a hike. The ground is so hot. On a day like this, frogs wear shoes!"

"They do?" Huey said.

"Especially if they go hiking," my father said. "Of course, a lot of frogs, on a day like this, would stay home. So I wonder why you kids are hiking."

Sometimes my father notices too much. Then he gets yellow lights shining in his eyes, asking you to tell the whole truth. That's when I know to look at my feet.

"Oh," I said, "we *like* hiking."

But Gloria didn't know any better. She looked into my father's eyes. "Really," she said, "this wasn't a real hike. We came to see you."

"Oh, I see!" my father said, looking pleased.

"Because we were bored," Huey said.

My father jumped up so fast he tipped over his lemonade cup. "BORED!" my father yelled. "You were BORED?"

He picked up his cup and waved it in the air.

"And you think *I* don't get BORED?" my father roared, sprinkling out a few last drops of lemonade from his cup. "You think I don't get bored fixing cars when it's hot enough that frogs wear shoes?"

" 'This is such an interesting world that nobody should ever be bored.' That's what you said," I reminded him.

"Last week," Huey added.

"Ummm," my father said. He got quiet.

He rubbed his hand over his mouth, the way he does when he's thinking.

"Why, of course," my father said, "I remember that. And it's the perfect, absolute truth. People absolutely SHOULD NOT get bored! However—" He paused. "It just happens that, sometimes, they do."

My father rubbed a line in the dirt with his shoe. He was thinking so hard I could see his thoughts standing by the tree and sitting on all the fenders of the cars.

"You know, if you three would kindly help me some more, I could leave a half hour early, and we could drive down by the river."

"We'll help," I said.

"Yes, and then we can look for frogs!" Huey said. So we stayed. We learned how to make a signal light blink. And afterward, on the way to the river, my dad bought us all ice cream cones. The ice cream did melt. Huey's melted all down the front of his shirt. It took him ten paper napkins and the river to clean up.

A Day When Frogs Wear Shoes 241

After Huey's shirt was clean, we took our shoes and socks off and went wading.

We looked for special rocks under the water—the ones that are beautiful until you take them out of the water, when they get dry and not so bright.

We found skipping stones and tried to see who could get the most skips from a stone.

We saw a school of minnows going as fast as they could to get away from us.

But we didn't see any frogs.

"If you want to see frogs," my father said, "you'll have to walk down the bank a ways and look hard."

So we decided to do that.

"Fine!" my father said. "But I'll stay here. I think I'm ready for a little nap."

"Naps are boring!" we said.

"Sometimes it's nice to be bored," my father said.

We left him with his eyes closed, sitting under a tree.

Huey saw the first frog. He almost stepped on it. It jumped into the water, and we ran after it.

A Day When Frogs Wear Shoes 243

Huey caught it and picked it up, and then I saw another one. I grabbed it.

It was slippery and strong and its body was cold, just like it wasn't the middle of summer. Then Gloria caught one too. The frogs wriggled in our hands, and we felt their hearts beating. Huey looked at their funny webbed feet.

"Their feet are good for swimming," he said, "but Dad is wrong. They don't wear shoes!"

"No way," Gloria said. "They sure don't wear shoes."

"Let's go tell him," I said.

We threw our frogs back into the river. They made little trails swimming away from us. And then we went back to my father.

He was sitting under the tree with his eyes shut. It looked like he hadn't moved an inch.

"We found frogs," Huey said, "and we've got news for you. They don't wear shoes!"

My father's eyes opened. "They don't?" he said. "Well, I can't be right about everything. Dry your feet. Put your shoes on. It's time to go."

We all sat down to put on our shoes.

I pulled out a sock and put it on.

I stuck my foot into my shoe. My foot wouldn't go in.

I picked up the shoe and looked inside.

"Oh no!" I yelled.

There were two little eyes inside my shoe, looking out at me. Huey and Gloria grabbed their socks. All our shoes had frogs in them, every one.

"What did I tell you," my father said.

"You were right," we said. "It's a day when frogs wear shoes!"

About the Author

When **Ann Cameron** was in third grade, she decided she wanted to be a writer. Today, children around the world have read her *Julian* books, originally inspired by stories that a friend, Julian DeWette, told her about his childhood. One time, Ms. Cameron wanted to write about Julian and Huey taking a river trip with their father. When she sat down to write, however, her idea suddenly seemed boring. It was a cold winter day, and Ms. Cameron began imagining how hot the hottest day would be. She ended up with *A Day When Frogs Wear Shoes*!

A Day When Frogs Wear Shoes

Whether the weather be fine,
Or whether the weather be not,
Whether the weather be cold,
Or whether the weather be hot,
We'll weather the weather
Whatever the weather,
Whether we like it or not!

Weather

Anonymous

Studying the Selection

FIRST IMPRESSIONS
What can you do to turn a hot, boring day into a day to remember?

QUICK REVIEW

1. Why were the three children sitting on the front steps?
2. Why was visiting Dad a "dangerous" idea?
3. What expression did Dad use to describe how hot it was?
4. What did the children find in their shoes at the end of the day?

FOCUS

5. The nice thing about Dad was that he let the kids feel both grown up and like kids. Which things did the children do that made them feel grown up? Which things did they do that let them feel like kids?
6. Dad was a very caring father. He wanted the kids to have confidence, so he gave them jobs and praised them when they did them well. A second trait he wanted them to have was to be able to relax and enjoy the world around them. What did Dad do to help the children develop this trait?

CREATING AND WRITING

7. Everyone has had a day with nothing to do. It might have been a rainy day in summer, or a cold day in winter. It might have been a day when you were sick, or a day when none of your friends could play. Write a short story about what you did to change a day from boring to fun. The story may be true or made up—just so long as it's interesting!

8. The English language is full of colorful expressions. Every generation has its own. Here are a few examples:
   - That name rings a bell.
   - Bite your tongue!
   - She's got a sunny smile.

   Do you know any? Choose an expression that you know or one from a list your teacher will provide and draw a picture of it. Under the picture, write the expression.

Lesson in Literature
The Grandmother

CAUSE AND EFFECT
- A **cause** is something that makes another thing happen. (Joe *hit* the ball.)
- An **effect** is what happens due to a cause. (The window was *broken* by the ball.)
- In a story, sometimes the author will start with a cause and end with an effect.
- In a story, sometimes the author will start with an effect and end with a cause. (Mrs. Wilkins woke up to find her window broken. What had caused it to break?)

THINK ABOUT IT!
1. What caused the people in the town to try hard not to criticize others or say mean things about other people?
2. What would be the effect of the War on all the people?
3. What was the effect that Grandma's kindness had on the generals?

Not so long ago, there lived a grandmother in a town not far away. Her husband was no longer alive, but she had several grown-up children and many grandchildren. She was wise and kind, good to friends and strangers alike. It was almost as if she were everyone's grandmother. In fact, all of the people in the town called her Grandma.

Her children and grandchildren had learned from her. They each helped their neighbors whenever there was a need. They tried hard not to criticize others or to say mean things about other people. They had great respect for Grandma and wanted to be like her.

Then, war came to the land. The War was being fought between the Northerners and the Southerners. There were no newspapers or radios or telephones in the town, but eventually the townspeople got word of the conflict. Because the town was located mostly in the South, the townsfolk declared that they would stand with the Southerners.

Grandma said little about the War, except to shake her head sadly and say softly, "What a pity!" Although some of the reasons for the War were very important, the fighting would cause great suffering for many people. How much better it would have been if the struggle between the North and South had been solved peacefully!

Grandma was surprised to see that some of her own children and grandchildren were excited by the War. Most of them were cheering for the South to win. Grandma said quietly to her oldest daughter, "Don't they know that even when you win a war, you still lose?" Nonetheless, several of her younger sons and her older grandsons went off to fight in the Southern Army.

Some of the townspeople thought that Grandma didn't take one side or the other because she was getting old and becoming less wise. Others thought it was because Grandma's cabin was located exactly halfway in the North and halfway in the South.

As the War went on, there was news that many young men had lost their lives in the fighting. As the fighting came closer to the town, people approached Grandma and declared, "Grandma, you have to take a side! You have to be for the South." Grandma remained silent.

That afternoon, Grandma called all of her daughters to her cabin. She told them that they needed to put all other chores aside. They must begin making loaves of bread, filling up available bottles with water from the well, and finally, tearing cloth for bandages. The daughters and grandchildren set to work right away.

When neighbors heard about this, they, too, baked bread, got water, and made bandages. Soon, the whole town was busy.

Six days later, the battle arrived nearly at Grandma's front door. In the field across the road, the soldiers fought. But stored in Grandma's cabin, there were more than a hundred loaves of bread, fifty bottles of water, and piles of bandages.

The fighting was terrible. It lasted for many hours. When it was over, hundreds of wounded soldiers from North and South lay about the field. They called for water. They called for their mothers. They called for their wives. The cries that came from the injured Northerners were no different from the cries that came from the injured Southerners.

Grandma gathered her children and grandchildren together. For once, she spoke very loudly. "It is time to go and give aid. You will not choose between North and South. We help every young man out there."

When word of Grandma's kindness reached the generals of the Northern and Southern armies, each side sent a regiment of soldiers to guard Grandma's house for the remainder of the War.

Blueprint for Reading

INTO . . . *The Burning of the Rice Fields*

What is a hero? Many different qualities go into making a hero, but one stands out from the rest. That quality is the ability to put someone else's needs before one's own. The firefighter who runs into a burning building to save people is a good example: he is putting someone else's life before his own. A person need not be strong to be a hero—the person must be *selfless*, which means sacrificing one's own needs for the sake of someone or something else. A hero might be an elderly wife caring for her sick husband; it could be a poor child sharing her lunch with another poor child.

As you read *The Burning of the Rice Fields*, you will get to know a man who is a true hero.

EYES ON *Cause and Effect*

What is **cause and effect**? It is easiest to explain with an example. If you throw a snowball at your neighbor's window and the window breaks, your snowball is the *cause* and the broken window is the *effect*. But cause and effect don't even have to be physical; they can also be words or thoughts. For example, imagine that a boy named Jack says something mean to his classmate, Mike, and Mike feels bad. The *cause* is Jack's mean words and the *effect* is Mike's hurt feelings.

As you read *The Burning of the Rice Fields*, you may try to predict the effect Hamaguchi's actions will have. You will wonder: Why is he doing this terrible thing? If you are surprised by the answer, you won't be the only reader who is—which is what makes this such a good story!

The Burning of the Rice Fields

Lafcadio Hearn

Far away in Japan, many years ago, lived good old Hamaguchi.[1] He was the wisest man of his village, and the people loved and honored him.

Hamaguchi was a wealthy farmer. His farmhouse stood on a hillside high above the seashore. Down by the shore, and scattered up the hill, were the houses of his neighbors. Around his own house the ground was flat, like the top of a huge step in the hillside, and all about him stretched his rice fields.

1. *Hamaguchi* (HA ma GOO chee)

It was the time of harvest. Hundreds of rice stacks lined Hamaguchi's fields. It had been a fine harvest, and tonight down in the village everyone was having a good time.

Hamaguchi sat outside his house and looked down into the village. He would have liked to join the other villagers, but he was too tired—the day had been very hot. So he stayed at home with his little grandson, Tada. They could see the flags and the paper lanterns that hung across the streets of the village, and see the people getting ready for the dance. The low sun lighted up all the moving bits of color below.

It was still very hot, though a strong breeze was beginning to blow in from the sea. Suddenly the hillside shook—just a little, as if a wave were rolling slowly under it. The house creaked and rocked gently for a moment. Then all became still again.

"An earthquake," thought Hamaguchi, "but not very near. The worst of it seems far away."

Hamaguchi was not frightened, for he had felt the earth quake many a time before. Yet he looked anxiously toward the village. Then, suddenly, he rose to his feet and looked out at the sea. The sea was very dark, and, strange to say, it seemed to be running away from the land.

    Soon all the village had noticed how the water was rolling out. The people hurried down to the beach. Not one of them had ever seen such a thing before.

    For a moment, on the hillside, Hamaguchi stood and looked. Then he called, "Tada! Quick—very quick! Light me a torch!"

Tada ran into the house and picked up one of the torches that stood ready for use on stormy nights. He lighted it and ran back to his grandfather. Quickly the old man grabbed the torch and hurried to the rice fields. Tada ran with him, wondering what he was going to do.

When they reached the first row of rice stacks, Hamaguchi ran along the row, touching the torch to each stack as he passed. The rice was dry, and the fire caught quickly. The seabreeze, blowing stronger, began to drive the flames ahead. Row after row, the stacks caught fire. Soon flames and smoke towered up against the sky.

Tada ran after his grandfather, crying, "Grandfather, why? Why?"

Had his grandfather gone mad? Why was he burning the rice that was their food and all their wealth? But Hamaguchi went on from stack to stack, till he reached the end of the field. Then he threw down his torch and waited.

The bell-ringer in the tower on the hill saw the flames and set the big bell booming. And, down on the beach, the people turned and began to climb the hill. If Hamaguchi's rice fields were afire, nothing would keep them from helping him.

First up the hill came some of the young men, who wanted to fight the fire at once. But Hamaguchi stood in front of the fields and held out his hands to stop them.

"Let it burn," he ordered. "Let it burn."

Soon the whole village was coming. Men and boys, women and girls, mothers with babies on their backs, and even little children came. Children could help pass buckets of water.

Still Hamaguchi stood in front of his burning fields and waited. Meanwhile the sun went down.

The people began to question Tada. What had happened? Why wouldn't his grandfather let them fight the fire? Was he mad?

"I don't know," cried Tada, for he was really frightened. "Grandfather set fire to the rice on purpose. I saw him do it!"

"Yes," cried Hamaguchi. "I set fire to the rice. Are all the people here now?"

The villagers looked about them. Then they answered, "All are here, but we do not understand—"

The Burning of the Rice Fields   257

"Look!" shouted Hamaguchi, as loud as he could. He was pointing to the sea. "Look! Now do you think I have gone mad?"

All turned and looked toward the sea. Far, far out, where the sea and sky seem to meet, stretched a cloudy line that came nearer and nearer. It was the sea coming back to the shore. But it towered like a great wall of rock. It rolled more swiftly than a kite could fly.

"The sea!" screamed the people. Hardly had they spoken, when the great wall of water struck the shore. The noise was louder than any thunder. The hillside shook. A sheet of foam was dashed far up to where the people stood.

When the sea went back, not a house was left below them on the hillside or along the shore. The whole village had been swept away.

The people stood silent, too frightened to speak. Then they heard Hamaguchi saying gently, "That is why I set fire to the rice ... My house still stands, and there is room for many. The tower on the hill still stands. There is shelter there for the rest."

Then the people woke, as if from a dream, and understood. Hamaguchi had made himself poor to save them, and they realized how great a man he was.

About the Author

When **Lafcadio Hearn** was born in Greece in 1850, his parents named him Patricio Lafcadio Tessima Carlos Hearn. Mr. Hearn grew up in Ireland and went to school in England. When he was 19 years old, he came to America. In America, he worked in a library for a short time, but he was fired because he spent too much time reading instead of working. When Mr. Hearn was 40 years old, he moved to Japan, where he changed his name to Koizumi Yakumo and wrote many books about Japan.

The Burning of the Rice Fields

UNTIL I SAW THE SEA

Lilian Moore

Until I saw the sea
I did not know
that wind
could wrinkle water so.

I never knew
that sun
could splinter a whole sea of blue.

Nor
did I know before,
a sea breathes in and out
upon a shore.

Studying the Selection

FIRST IMPRESSIONS
Do you remember Tassai and her split-second decision? Here's someone else who must decide in one moment whether or not to give up all his wealth. Are you good at making big decisions? What about little ones?

QUICK REVIEW
1. Why was Hamaguchi a wealthy man?
2. Why were the villagers celebrating that night?
3. What did Hamaguchi see that shocked him?
4. Why did Hamaguchi set fire to the fields?

FOCUS
5. Hamaguchi showed that he was very smart; he knew just how to get the villagers to run from the village. Another trait Hamaguchi had was that he was decisive. He made decisions quickly and acted upon them. What important decision does Hamaguchi make and carry out?
6. Tada was so loyal to Hamaguchi, that he always obeyed him without questioning him. How did this trait help Hamaguchi's plan succeed?

CREATING AND WRITING
7. The author describes the huge wave that destroyed the village by comparing it to things with which we are familiar. He writes, *it towered like a great wall of rock. It rolled more swiftly than a kite could fly*. Close your eyes and picture a huge wave. If you were an author, how would *you* describe it? Write three sentences in which you compare the giant wave to something else that helps the reader feel its power.
8. The village below Hamaguchi's house would have to be rebuilt. What does a new village need? Your teacher will divide your class into groups and give each group a poster board. Each group will draw their idea of what the new village will look like. Before you begin drawing the village, write a list of the shops and buildings you will include.

Lesson in Literature...
Betsy Brotman in Liberia

What is Biography?
- A **biography** is the true story of a person's life.
- A biography may take the form of a short story, a full-length book, or even a drama.
- A biography may cover the entire life of a person or may tell about only one part of the person's life.
- A good biography will tell only the facts about a person's life and allow the reader to form an opinion about that person.

Think About It!
1. What work did Betsy come to Liberia to do, and who had hired her to do it?
2. How did Betsy and her husband treat the chimps? Bring a few examples of the way they treated the chimps.
3. From a person's actions, one can learn about the character traits this person has. Name one character trait that Betsy had, and write down how you know that she had that trait.

In 1974, Betsy Brotman arrived in Robertsfield, Liberia. She had come to the West African country from the United States. She was 32 and was going to do research on diseases.

Betsy was the director of the Liberian Biomedical Research Institute. The land set aside for the Institute was called a compound. The compound on which Betsy and her family lived became home to 150 chimpanzees, many cats, several dogs, a pig, a warthog, a mongoose, two baby leopards, and two dik-diks. Dik-diks are very tiny antelope.

The compound included the big house (in which Betsy, her daughter, and her husband, Brian, lived), a house for the veterinarian, a large laboratory, many clean, spacious cages for the chimps, and many smaller guesthouses for visitors. The big house was set on stilts, because of the floods that occurred during the rainy season.

Betsy's home was like a hotel for people visiting Liberia. All of the pilots and flight attendants who flew on planes to Liberia from Europe and the United States visited Betsy. People who worked for foreign companies became good friends, as did the ambassadors from other countries.

Betsy worked very hard to organize the Institute and to do research that would help human beings. She loved the animals. Every chimp had a name and Betsy knew all 150 of them. The mongoose was called "Goosie," and lived in the big house. Of course the dogs and cats were allowed to sleep inside. The warthog came as a baby, and slept in the living room until he weighed 200 lbs.

Two of the chimps were babies. Fat Fanny Foo-Foo and Evelyn were kept in diapers and lived in the house. As infants, they were bottle-fed. As they got older, they wore little dresses and ate at the table with spoons and forks.

There were several bad wars in Liberia while Betsy lived there. During the wars, her daughter went to live with Betsy's parents in the United States. Betsy and Brian would not leave, because they wanted to protect the chimpanzees from the soldiers.

In the late 1980s, Betsy realized that the chimpanzees needed to be reintroduced to the wild. If a time came when they could no longer live on the compound, they would have to know how to take care of themselves. For a long time she tried to get the governments of other African countries interested in taking them. But in spite of many promises that were made, the chimps remained in Liberia on the compound. Finally, she persuaded some of the officials in Liberia to let her use two islands for the chimps' home.

She and her husband and their helpers took some of the chimps in boats to the islands. Every day, they took a boat full of mangoes, and went down the river to feed the chimps. The chimps were unable to learn how to find food after being cared for for so many years.

One night, one of the big male chimps went over to the other island and killed another chimp. Betsy realized that they would have to dig a much deeper canal between the two islands. One of the drug companies for whom she was doing research agreed to pay for the digging.

While she was in Liberia, Betsy did not only adopt chimpanzees, a mongoose, and a warthog. She adopted four children, raised them, and they now live in the U.S. Sadly, her husband Brian died in 1993 during one of the wars.

Betsy left Liberia for good in 2009. She had spent a long time there, and she did not want to leave. The company that she had worked for all of those years no longer wanted to do medical research. She left behind the 63 chimpanzees that had somehow survived the many years of war.

Blueprint for Reading

INTO . . . *Mother to Tigers*

Have you ever cared for a small animal? Have you ever nursed an injured bird back to health? If you have, then you know how much time, effort, and love goes into caring for a kitten that doesn't have a mother or a bird with a broken wing. How did you feel when your "patient" began to heal? Here is a story about a woman who, with the help of her husband, took many different baby animals from the zoo into her home. She kept them there until they were ready to go back to the zoo. The woman put all of her heart into healing the sickly animals. What was her reward? As you read *Mother to Tigers*, you will find out.

EYES ON *Biography*

A **biography** is a story about a real person. It can describe part or all of a person's life. The events and characters are all real. Sometimes, when we read about a person who was exceptionally good we become *inspired*. That means that we are impressed with what that person has done, and would like to do the same. As you read this short biography, you will feel inspired by Helen Frances Theresa Delaney Martini. Why? You will know after you have read only a bit of *Mother to Tigers*.

Mother to Tigers

GEORGE ELLA LYON

Suppose you were a lion cub—abandoned.
Suppose you lay hungry and cold
in the straw at the back of the den,

and a man came in the cage
and lifted you into a case

and put you in a car
to go home with him.

WORD BANK

abandoned (uh BAN dund) *adj.*: left to manage on its own; deserted

Suppose a woman bathed you.
Suppose she warmed milk on the stove
and poured it in a bottle
and put you on a pillow in her lap
to drink till you were full and sleepy,

then put you in a box that would be your bed
in a kitchen that would be your home

till you got big enough to roam the apartment,
stalking the sofa, pouncing on the chairs,
till you outgrew a human's house
and went home to the Bronx Zoo.

Your name would be MacArthur,
and the woman who saved you,
Helen Frances Theresa Delaney Martini.

Helen never planned to raise cubs.
She and her husband, Fred, wanted children.
But their first baby died,
and doctors said she couldn't have more.

To ease their hurt hearts,
they collected pets: a parrot, a dog,
a starling,[1] and twelve canaries.

Before long, their little apartment
was full of song and feathers.

---
1. A *starling* is a shiny, black songbird.

Word Bank

roam (ROME) *v.*: to wander all around

pouncing (POWN sing) *v.*: swooping down on suddenly

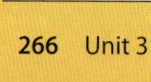

266 Unit 3

Mother to Tigers 267

On weekends, when Fred was free
from his job as a jeweler,
they strolled through the Bronx Zoo,
just down the street from their house.

Fred loved those times—
watching polar bears dive
and elephants amble,
studying the grace of giraffes.
Finally Helen said,
"Why don't you follow your heart
and work at the Zoo?"
So he did.

Each night he brought home questions
about animals he cared for,
and together he and Helen would read and learn.

When he brought MacArthur home
to the apartment on Old Kingsbridge Road,
the cub was a pitiful sight.
"Just do for him what you would do
for a human baby," Fred told Helen.
And she did.

Word Bank

strolled *v.*: walked in a casual way, without hurrying

grace *n.*: smooth and beautiful movements

pitiful (PIH tih FULL) *adj.*: causing one to feel pity

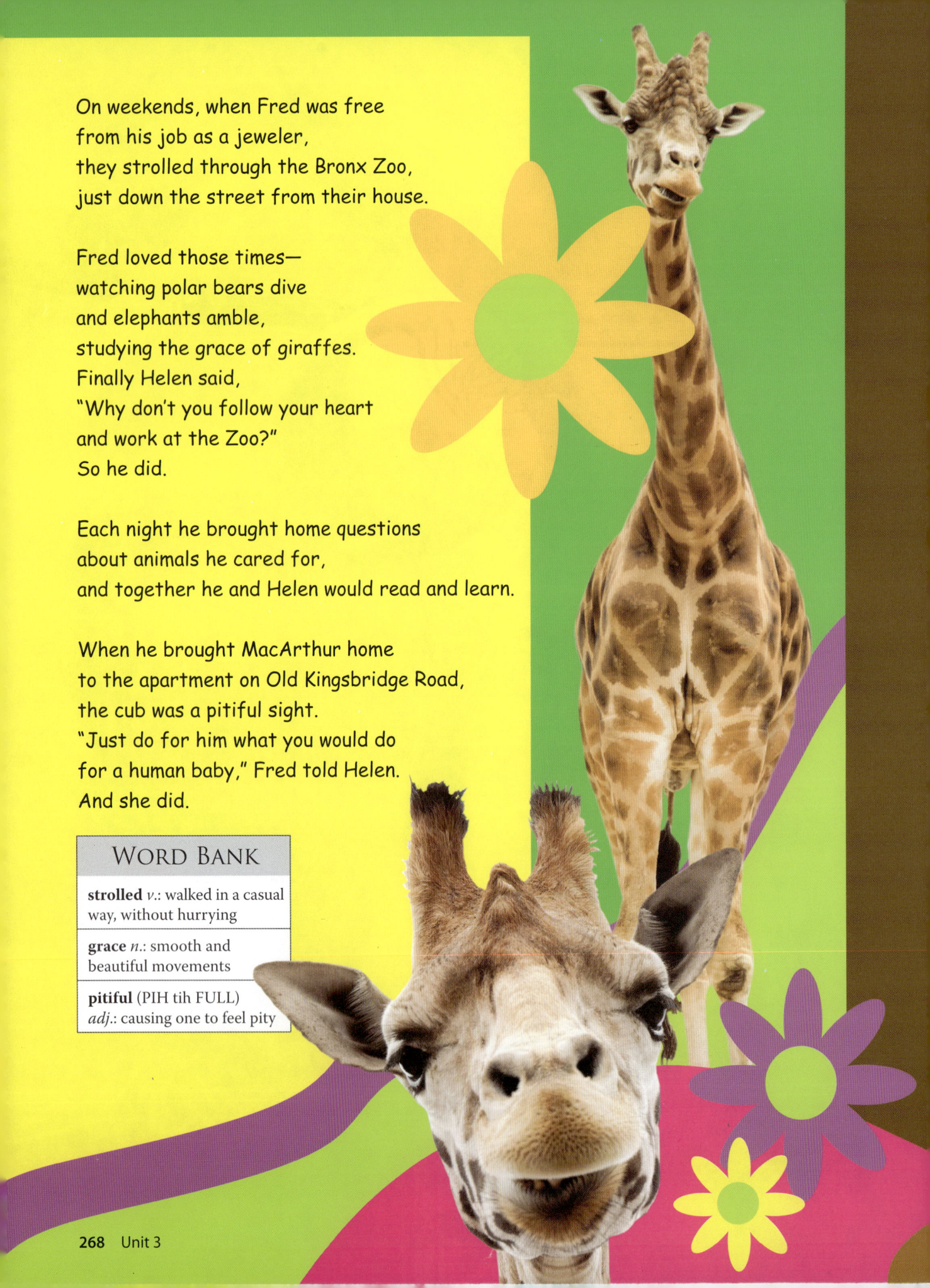

Mother to Tigers 269

270 Unit 3

After MacArthur
came Dacca,[2] Rajpur,[3] and Raniganj,[4]
a litter of Bengal tigers.

Rajpur was so cold and thin,
Helen thought he might die,
but she put him on a heating pad
and sat by him for hours
moistening his mouth with milk.
At last he gave a weak cry.
Helen almost cried too.

Feeding three was a challenge!
Helen wished she were an octopus.
But before long those scrawny babies
were sleek, fat cubs, ready to romp.

Once, washing clothes in the bath,
Helen heard Raniganj crying.
His head was caught behind a pipe.
While she ran to the rescue,

Rajpur and Dacca discovered the tub.
Crouch … leap … *splash*!
Tigers love water.

---
2. *Dacca* (DAHK KAH)
3. *Rajpur* (raj POOR)
4. *Raniganj* (rah NEE GUNJ)

Word Bank
challenge (CHAL unj) *n.*: a test of one's abilities
sleek *adj.*: well-fed and looking fit
crouch *v.*: to bend low close to the ground preparing to leap

When the striped trio
had to go back to the Zoo,
they still needed their bottles,
so Helen brought a hot plate
and set up a little kitchen
in the sleeping room
at the back of their cage.

The first night, she and Fred
ate their dinner there too.
Helen didn't want to leave
till her cubs were fast asleep.

Come daybreak, she was back
and she was thinking:
These tigers will grow up,
but there will always be zoo babies
who need special care.
She couldn't take all of them home,
but she could bring home to them.
She could start a nursery at the Zoo!

"Just give me a room," she said
to Mr. Crandall, the man in charge.
"I'll do all the work."
And she did.

She cleaned and plastered a storeroom,
which she painted pink and blue.

Then she begged, borrowed, and bought
everything she needed.

Starting out, she didn't get paid,
but that wasn't what mattered.
She was following her heart,
and her nursery filled up quickly.

Soon it was official:
She was the first woman keeper
in the history of the Bronx Zoo.

Before Helen arrived,
no tiger born at the Zoo had ever survived.
   She raised twenty-seven,

Word Bank

official (uh FISH ul) *adj.*: approved by the people in charge

along with yapoks[5] and marmosets,[6]
gorillas and chimpanzees,
deer and ring-tailed lemurs.[7]

She still took cubs home, too:
lions, tigers,
jaguars, and a black leopard.

Helen's cubs had cubs
that were sent to zoos
all around the world.
The idea of the nursery spread too.

So, wherever you live,
when you go to the zoo,
look hard at the mighty cats.

Their grandparents
may have opened their eyes
on Old Kingsbridge Road,

may have learned to walk
in that apartment kitchen,

saved
by Helen Frances Theresa Delaney Martini,
mother to tigers.

---

5. A *yapok* (JAH pock), sometimes called a water opossum, is a gray opossum with dark bands on its fur. It lives on land and water.
6. *Marmosets* are monkeys that are about the size of squirrels.
7. *Lemurs* (LEE murs) are small, cat-like animals who have large eyes, fox-like faces, and long tails.

ABOUT THE AUTHOR

George Ella Lyon grew up in a house with a room just for books. She remembers building mazes out of books before she could read. Mrs. Lyon is named "George" after her mother's brother. As a child, she wanted to be a zookeeper. When she was 10 years old, she read a book by Helen Martini about her experiences raising lion and tiger cubs. This book sparked Mrs. Lyon's interest in big cats, particularly lions. Mrs. Lyon says that although she never became a zookeeper, she did end up marrying a Lyon.

Dreamer

Langston Hughes

I take my dreams

And make of them a bronze vase,

And a wide round fountain

With a beautiful statue in its center,

And a song with a broken heart,

And I ask you:

Do you understand my dreams?

Sometimes you say you do

And sometimes you say you don't.

Either way

It doesn't matter.

I continue to dream.

Studying the Selection

FIRST IMPRESSIONS
When you hear the word "mother," what traits do you think of? When you hear that someone is called "Mother to Tigers," what do you think is her connection to tigers?

QUICK REVIEW
1. Why did Helen and her husband start to take care of pets?
2. How did Helen know what to do for the first sick cub Fred brought home?
3. What did Helen do so that she could continue to care for the animals she'd nursed back to health once they returned to the zoo?
4. What did Helen achieve that no one before her had?

FOCUS
5. What do you think was the hardest part of Helen's job?
6. Helen had many wonderful character traits. One of them was that she was a very hard worker. Another trait was that when something didn't go her way, she didn't give up; she tried something else. Write three sentences about someone you know who has one of these traits and how that person uses it.

CREATING AND WRITING
7. A zookeeper keeps logs of the progress of every animal in the zoo. Imagine that you are Helen and you have just taken home a baby tiger cub who is underweight, hardly moves, and has an eye infection. For the next seven days you will keep a log that records the cub's condition, what you fed it, what medicine you gave it, and what improvement you see. You will make up this information. Your teacher will give you instructions to help you make the chart.
8. Baby animals are magical! Together, your class will make a border they can put on the wall to liven up your classroom. If you can find pictures of baby animals at home, bring them in. Your teacher will supply you with some more pictures, and a cardboard border. Each student will cut out a picture of one baby animal and glue it to the border. When the border is complete, your teacher will hang it up.

unit 3 wrap-up

all about characters!

ACTIVITY ONE

Sometimes, when a theater group puts on a performance, they sell souvenirs of the play they are performing. For example, if a theater were presenting a play about "the cat in the hat," they might sell big hats as souvenirs of the play. A souvenir could be a pin, a bag, a T-shirt, or a variety of other things. Imagine that you are part of a group that is performing one of the stories in this unit as a play. Choose one of the stories and, using materials provided by your teacher, create a souvenir for it.

The Printer

Lorenzo & Angelina

A Day When Frogs Wear Shoes

The Burning of the Rice Fields

Mother to Tigers

HERO

ACTIVITY TWO

Your town is holding a contest to select a hero from amongst the townspeople. The hero is awarded a prize. They do this every year to show appreciation for the hero's good deeds and to inspire everyone else. This year, the choices have been narrowed down to two heroes. The first is the father from the story, *The Printer*, who saved the lives of all the printers by alerting them to the fire in the shop. The second is Hamaguchi from the story, *The Burning of the Rice Fields*, who saved the townspeople from being drowned by a tidal wave. Everyone in town has been asked to cast a vote for the hero of their choice. Decide who you would choose as the winner. Write a paragraph that you will read to the class in which you say why you think your choice of hero should win the prize.

Unit 3 Wrap-Up

Unit 3 wrap-up continued

280　Unit 3

ACTIVITY THREE

Let's play Memory! On cards that your teacher will give you, draw a picture of a scene or a character from one of the stories in this unit. Draw the same picture on a second card. After everyone has created two matching cards, your teacher will divide your class into groups of seven or eight. Each group will take the cards its members have drawn, mix them up, and spread them out face down. Following the rules of the game, Memory, take turns trying to find pairs. The student in each group who has the most pairs of cards is the winner.

ACTIVITY FOUR

It is a summer day and, once again, the three children in *A Day When Frogs Wear Shoes* are bored. This time, Ralph, the father of two of the children, has a plan. He is going to take them to the zoo. At the zoo, the group meets Helen the zookeeper (from *Mother to Tigers*), and she shows them her nursery of young, weak animals. The children immediately ask if they can take one of the tiger cubs home and nurse him back to health. Dad is not very eager to do this, and Helen is concerned that the children will not know what to do with the cub.

Write a conversation between the children (you can use their names: Huey, Gloria, and Julian, the narrator), Dad, and Helen in which they discuss whether or not the children should take home the cub. You will probably want to have Dad asking questions, the children insisting that they can do the job, and Helen giving warnings and instructions. The conversation, or dialogue, should be from six to eight lines long. To show who is speaking, write the speaker's name followed by a colon (:) and then the words that he or she says. Whenever a new character begins to speak, start another line.

Unit 3 Wrap-Up   281

Mosdos Press
Literature

- **GLOSSARY**
- **ACKNOWLEDGMENTS**
- **INDEX OF AUTHORS AND TITLES**

glossary

A

abandoned (uh BAN dund) *adj.*: left to manage on its own; deserted

apothecary (uh PAH thuh keh ree) *n.*: a pharmacy

B

beams *n.*: thick, strong boards that go across the width of a ship

blacksmith *n.*: a person who makes horseshoes and puts them on the horses

blossomed (BLAH sumd) *v.*: grew and developed tremendously

brayed *v.*: sounded the harsh cry of the donkey

burro (BURR oh) *n.*: a small donkey used to carry loads

C

challenge (CHAL unj) *n.*: a test of one's abilities

coaxed (KOKST) *v.*: gently tried to get someone to do something

cooper *n.*: a person who makes or repairs barrels or tubs

crouch *v.*: to bend low close to the ground preparing to leap

D

desperate (DESS prit) *adj.*: extremely needy

E

engulfed (en GULFD) *v.*: completely swallowed up

enthusiastic (en THOOZ ee AS tik) *adj.*: excited and eager

exchanged (ex CHANGED) *v.*: traded

F

fled *v.*: run away from

furrows *n.*: narrow grooves made in the ground

G

grace *n.*: smooth and beautiful movements

H

hauling (HAWL ing) *v.*: pulling

I

image (IH muj) *n.*: picture in one's mind

independence (IN dih PEN dunce) *n.*: freedom; the right to think and act for oneself

Glossary 283

glossary

J

jauntily (JAWN tih lee) *adv.*: worn easily, happily, and a tiny bit proudly

L

lariat (LARE ee ut) *n.*: lasso; a long, noosed rope used to catch horses, cattle, or other livestock

livery (LIH vuh ree) *n.*: a place where horses are cared for, fed, and stabled for pay

M

midst *n.*: the middle of

miller *n.*: a person who grinds grain into flour

miraculously (mih RAK yuh luss lee) *adv.*: as though through a miracle

N

numb (NUM) *adj.*: without any feeling at all

O

official (uh FISH ul) *adj.*: approved by the people in charge

P

pitiful (PIH tih FULL) *adj.*: causing one to feel pity

plucked *v.*: pulled out with force

poncho (PAHN cho) *n.*: a cloak that has an opening in the middle so that it can be pulled over the head and worn around the body

pouncing (POWN sing) *v.*: swooping down on suddenly

prospector (PROSS pek ter) *n.*: a person who searches and digs for gold in certain areas

R

radiator (RAY dee AY ter) *n.*: a room heater made of pipes through which steam or hot water passes

raging (RAY jing) *adj.*: angry and dangerous

roam (ROME) *v.*: to wander all around

S

scarcely (SKAIRS lee) *adv.*: hardly

settlement (SET ul ment) *n.*: the beginnings of a town; a group of houses built in a new, unsettled area

shafts *n.*: long columns

shuddered (SHUH derd) *v.*: shook slightly

skillet *n.*: frying pan

sleek *adj.*: well-fed and looking fit

glossary

spewing (SPYOO ing) *v.*: throwing out with force

stagecoach *n.*: a horse-drawn coach that carried passengers, mail, and packages

strained *v.*: tried to make them work even better than they usually did

strolled *v.*: walked in a casual way, without hurrying

T

tanner *n.*: a person who makes leather out of animal hides

thicket (THIK it) *n.*: a group of bushes or small trees growing closely together

V

vast *adj.*: huge; covering a very great area

acknowledgments

Illustrators
Sharon Bunting: Sybil Rides By Night
Eva Clair: A Cane in Her Hand; Boom Town; Across the Wide Dark Sea; Lorenzo & Angelina; The Burning of the Rice Fields; The Secret; The Other Way to Listen

Aviva Goldfarb: The Jar of Tassai
Lydia Martin: The Story of the White Sombrero; Taro and the Tofu
Julie Orelowitz: A Day When Frogs Wear Shoes

Across the Wide Dark Sea
ACROSS THE WIDE DARK SEA text copyright © 1995 by Jean Van Leeuwen. Published in the United States by Dial Books for Young Readers. All rights reserved. Used with permission.

Boom Town
From BOOM TOWN by Sonia Levitin. Copyright © 1998 by Sonia Levitin. Reprinted by permission of Orchard Books, an imprint of Scholastic Inc.

Breakfast
"Breakfast", from THE OTHER SIDE OF THE DOOR by Jeff Moss, copyright © 1991 by Jeff Moss. Used by permission of Festival Attractions Inc.

A Cane in Her Hand
Text © Ada B. Litchfield, 1977; illustrations © Eleanor Mill, 1977. Published by Albert Whitman & Company. Used by permission.

A Day When Frogs Wear Shoes
"A Day When Frogs Wear Shoes" from MORE STORIES JULIAN TELLS by Ann Cameron, text copyright © 1986 by Ann Cameron. Used by permission of Alfred A. Knopf, an imprint of Random House Children's Books, a division of Penguin Random House LLC. All rights reserved.

Dreamer
"Dreamer" from THE COLLECTED POEMS OF LANGSTON HUGHES by Langston Hughes, edited by Arnold Rampersad with David Roessel, Associate Editor, copyright © 1994 by the Estate of Langston Hughes. Used by permission of Alfred A. Knopf, an imprint of the Knopf Doubleday Publishing Group, a division of Penguin Random House LLC. All rights reserved.

Food's on the Table
From ALL-OF-A-KIND FAMILY UPTOWN by Sydney Taylor, copyright © 1958, 1986 by Allenby & Co., LLC. No part of this excerpt may be reprinted in whole or in part without the express written permission of PearlCo Literary Agency, LLC.

General Store
"General Store," 1926 by Rachel Field, renewed 1953 by Arthur S. Pederson; from TAXIS AND TOADSTOOLS: VERSES AND DECORATIONS by Rachel Field. Used by permission of Doubleday, an imprint of Random House Children's Books, a division of Penguin Random House LLC. All rights reserved.

Good-Bye, 382 Shin Dang Dong
Reprinted by arrangement from the book *Good-Bye, 382 Shin Dang Dong*, by Frances Park and Ginger Park. Copyright © 2002 National Geographic Society.

I Am Running in a Circle
From THE NEW KID ON THE BLOCK by JACK PRELUTSKY. TEXT COPYRIGHT (C) 1984 BY JACK PRELUTSKY. Used by permission of HarperCollins Publishers.

I Go Forth to Move About the Earth
"I Go Forth to Move About the Earth" from WHISPERING WIND: POETRY BY YOUNG AMERICAN INDIANS by Terry Allen, copyright © 1972 by the Institute of American Indian Arts. Used by permission of Doubleday, an imprint of the Knopf Doubleday Publishing Group, a division of Penguin Random House LLC. All rights reserved.

Lorenzo & Angelina
Copyright © 1968 by Eugene Fern. Reprinted with permission of McIntosh & Otis, Inc.

Mother to Tigers
From **Mother to Tigers** by George Ella Lyon. Text copyright © 2003 George Ella Lyon. Reprinted with the permission of Atheneum Books for Young Readers, an imprint of Simon & Schuster Children's Publishing Division. All rights reserved.

New Kid at School
MESSING AROUND ON THE MONKEY BARS. Text copyright © 2009 Betsy Franco. Illustrations Copyright © 2009 Jessie Hartland. Reproduced by permission of the publisher, Candlewick Press, Somerville, MA.

Nothing Much Happened Today
Nothing Much Happened Today by Mary Blount Christian. Text copyright © 1973 by Mary Blount Christian. Reprinted by permission of the author.

The Other Way to Listen
From **The Other Way to Listen** by Byrd Baylor. Text copyright © 1978 by Byrd Baylor. Reprinted with the permission of Atheneum Books for Young Readers, an imprint of Simon & Schuster Children's Publishing Division. All rights reserved.

The Printer
First published in the United States under the title THE PRINTER by Myron Uhlberg, illustrated by Henri Sørensen. Text Copyright © 2003 by Myron Uhlberg, Illustrations Copyright © 2003 by Henri Sørensen. Published by arrangement with Peachtree Publishers.

Sybil Rides By Night
An excerpt from *Sybil Rides for Independence* by Drollene P. Brown. Copyright © 1985 by Drollene P. Brown. Reprinted by permission of the author.

Taro and the Tofu
Entire text from TARO AND THE TOFU by Masako Matsuno, text copyright © 1962, 1990 by Masako Matsuno. Used by permission of G. P. Putnam's Sons Books for Young Readers, an imprint of Penguin Young Readers Group, a division of Penguin Random House LLC. All rights reserved.

Until I Saw the Sea
From I FEEL THE SAME WAY by Lilian Moore. Copyright c 1967 C Renewed 1995. All Rights Reserved. Used by permission of Marian Reiner.

The World with its Countries
The World with its Countries by John Cotton. Copyright © 1989 by John Cotton. Reprinted by permission of the author.

Note: We have expended much effort to contact all copyright holders to receive permission to reprint their works. We will correct any omissions brought to our attention in future editions.

index of authors and titles

Italics indicates selection.

Roman indicates author biographical information.

Across the Wide Dark Sea, 163

Baylor, Byrd, 202

Boom Town, 53

Breakfast, 158

Brown, Drollene P., *121*, 130

Burning of the Rice Fields, The, 251

Cameron, Ann, *235*, 245

Cane in Her Hand, A, 39

Christian, Mary Blount, *135*, 143

Cotton, John, *178*

Day When Frogs Wear Shoes, A, 235

Dickinson, Emily, *16*

Dreamer, 276

Fern, Eugene, *213*, 230

Field, Rachel, 66

Food's on the Table, 149

Franco, Betsy, *116*

General Store, 66

Good-Bye, 382 Shin Dang Dong, 99

Hearn, Lafcadio, *251*, 258

Hughes, Langston, 276

I Am Running in a Circle, 144

I Go Forth to Move About the Earth, 48

Jar of Tassai, The, 5

Levitin, Sonia, *53*, 65

Litchfield, Ada B., *39*, 47

Lopez, Alonzo, *48*

Lorenzo & Angelina, 213

Lyon, George Ella, *265*, 275

Matsuno, Masako, *75*, 88

Moon, Grace, *5*, 15

Moore, Lilian, *260*

Moss, Jeff, *158*

Mother to Tigers, 265

New Kid at School, 116

Nothing Much Happened Today, 135

Other Way to Listen, The, 202

Park, Frances and Ginger, *99*, 115

Prelutsky, Jack, *144*

Prieto, Mariana, *21*, 34

Printer, The, 193

Secret, The, 16

Story of the White Sombrero, The, 21

Sybil Rides By Night, 121

Taro and the Tofu, 75

Taylor, Sydney, *149*, 157

Uhlberg, Myron, *193*, 199

Until I Saw the Sea, 260

Van Leeuwen, Jean, *163*, 177

Weather, 246

World with its Countries, The, 178